D1153863

The Culinary Institute of America
BOOK OF SOUPS

MORE THAN 100 NEW RECIPES FROM THE WORLD'S PREMIER CULINARY COLLEGE

The Culinary Institute of America

HYDE PARK, NEW YORK

Photography by Lorna Smith and Louis Wallach

LEBHAR-FRIEDMAN BOOKS

NEW YORK · CHICAGO · LOS ANGELES · LONDON · PARIS · TOKYO

THE CULINARY INSTITUTE OF AMERICA

Vice-President, Continuing Education: Mark Erickson

Director of Marketing and New Product Development: Sue Cussen

Director of Intellectual Property: Nathalie Fischer

Editors: Mary D. Donovan and Jennifer S. Armentrout

LEBHAR-FRIEDMAN BOOKS
A company of Lebhar-Friedman, Inc.
425 Park Avenue
New York, New York 10022

LIBRARY OF CONGRESS CATALOGING-IN-PUBLICATION DATA
Cataloging-in-publication data for this title is on file with the Library of Congress.
ISBN 0-86730-842-7 [978-0-86730-842-6 (hardcover)], 0-86730-858-3 [978-0-86730-858-7 (paperback)]

Designed and composed by Kevin Hanek; set in FF Scala and FF Scala Sans

Manufactured in Singapore by Imago Worldwide Printing on acid-free paper.

Visit our Web site at lfbooks.com

contents

introduction

FROM THE MOST DELICATE BROTH, through rib-sticking purees, and on to light, cool fruit soups, it is possible to find a soup to suit nearly any menu. Soups may serve as a single course of a meal, or they may be its centerpiece, rounded out with good bread and a green salad. If you are planning an elegant menu, soups make good starters, for many of them have just the subtle flavors to complement a complex main course. And, when you need a head start on satisfying meals for busy days, soups are a convenient answer, because most of them can be made when time allows and refrigerated or frozen until needed.

Soups can be among the best teachers of some important culinary lessons. They fill your mouth completely and instantly, giving you a simultaneous experience of aroma, texture, taste, and temperature. You can taste and evaluate soups at virtually any stage of preparation; if something starts to go awry, you can almost always fix it as you go.

Whether you are a beginner or an accomplished cook, soups are a good practice ground, for they rely on the most basic skills to prepare something truly delicious. Most soup recipes are extremely adaptable, and can be easily adjusted to meet the needs of the moment, particularly when you need to improvise ingredients. For example, a broth-based soup with lots of vegetables can usually accommodate a few beans or lentils for a more hearty main course soup. You can double, or even triple, most recipes to prepare some to eat now and some to freeze for later. As the great variety of recipes in this book shows, soup-making can transform virtually any nourishing ingredient into tempting fare.

This book includes 130 recipes, covering broths and light broth-based soups, hearty soups, pureed soups, cream soups, bisques, cold soups, and garnishes and accompaniments Chowders, borscht, and minestrone are included, along with many enduring favorites: cream of tomato, split pea, and French onion soup. The first part of several chapters also contains general illustrated methods for several "families" of soups to help you identify the relationships between different soups and gain confidence in your ability to improvise. Besides the chapters devoted to soup recipes, we have included a chapter devoted to the basics of ingredients, equipment, cooking, storing, and serving soups.

The recipes found in this book for such standards as chicken broth, cream of broccoli soup, and pureed bean soup can as a springboard into the wonderful soups enjoyed around the world. You can train your palate to memorize the gradual progression from the raw to the cooked, and learn to trust your cooking instincts as you begin to improvise. You will know that the season, the weather, the event, or a simple curiosity may send you off in a new direction. You will learn when and how to create variations, using classic practices gathered from the world's many cuisines. As you learn these and other valuable lessons in cooking for all the senses, you will also be rewarded with great soups.

acknowledgments

THE MAKING OF ANY BOOK IS A GROUP EFFORT. For their contributions in the making of this book, The Culinary Institute of America wishes to acknowledge the following individuals:

CULINARY CONTENT: Victor Gielisse, CMC, Associate Vice President of Culinary and Baking and Pastry Degree Programs; and Tim Ryan, CMC, Executive Vice President.

EDITORIAL: Mary Donovan, Senior Editor; Jennifer Armentrout, Editor; Jessica Bard, Photo Editor; and Mary Cowell, Director, The Food and Beverage Institute.

FOOD PREPARATION FOR PHOTOGRAPHY: Jessica Bard, Food/Prop Stylist; Chef Nancy Griffin; Kendra Glanbocky, Assistant Food/Prop Stylist; and Susan Ciriello, Margaret Hooker, and Juliana Santos, Chef's Assistants.

PHOTOGRAPHY: Lorna Smith and Louis Wallach, Photographers; Elizabeth Corbett Johnson, Photo Studio Manager; and Dennis Brandt, Christopher Fox, and Elizabeth Nicholson, Photographer's Assistants.

RECIPE TESTING: Lindsay Martin, Lynn McGillivray, Lisa Lahey, and Steven Wisniewski.

Special thanks to the faculty members of The Culinary Institute of America who contributed to the development of the basic methods and recipes for soups, as well as to Ania and Richard Aldrich of Rokeby Farm in Barrytown, New York, John and Jazzy Foreman of Daheim in Millbrook, New York, Elizabeth and Kevin Johnson of Rhinebeck, New York, and Mary Donovan and Thomas Schroeder of Red Hook, New York, for the use of their homes as locations for much of the photography in this book.

CHAPTER ONE

soup basics

INGREDIENTS ❖ EQUIPMENT ❖ COOKING ❖ ADJUSTING CONSISTENCY ❖ ADJUSTING

FLAVOR AND SEASONING ❖ COOLING AND STORING ❖ REHEATING ❖ SERVING

T HOUGH THE METHODS USED for making different soups vary, there are some general guidelines that apply to all soups. From ingredient and equipment selection through cooking, storing, and serving, this chapter will explore some of the basic principles of making soup.

INGREDIENTS

The long history of soup-making should reassure any cook that lack of the right ingredients is no deterrent to putting a pot on the stove. Indeed, soups are good storage vehicles for abundant harvests; freeze a bumper crop of tomatoes or cucumbers, for example, in soup form and you can be assured that nothing will go to waste.

The best soups are made from the best available ingredients. Since soups are mostly liquid, it stands to reason that the flavor of the liquid used to make the soup will strongly influence its overall flavor. If you start with a wonderful homemade broth, your soup will be distinguished by its fragrance. A very small number of soups call for so few ingredients other than broth that an insipid liquid will be quite noticeable. This is not to say, though, that commercially prepared broths and soup bases (see page 12) are never appropriate. These products are convenient and can be very necessary time savers under the right circumstances. Depending on the soup, they might be used as is, or you might choose to fortify and enhance their flavor first by simmering them with a few fresh aromatic ingredients (herbs, vegetables, etc.). Many soups are based on milk or the juices or cooking liquids of fresh fruits or vegetables. Still others are made with plain water to allow the flavor of the main ingredients to shine through.

The meats you choose for soup-making should be flavorful and mature. Generally, these cuts are the least expensive. Meats with a great deal of flavor, such as the neck, short ribs, hocks, or shank, are preferred for beef soups. Stewing hens are best for chicken-based soups. Fish or shellfish should be perfectly fresh.

Another important component is vegetables. The most frequently used vegetables are onions, leeks, carrots, and celery, but there are virtually no vegetables that cannot be included in a soup. Vegetable soups are an excellent way to use up wholesome odds and ends in your refrigerator, cooked or raw. Remember, though, that no soup can resurrect an over-the-hill ingredient. When you cut vegetables for soups, try to be as uniform as possible in the size of the pieces. The size affects the rate at which the vegetable will cook—evenly sized pieces will cook at the same speed.

Herbs, spices, and other aromatic ingredients (lemon grass or chiles, for example) are added to soups to increase flavor and, many times, to reduce or eliminate the need for salt. They are frequently tied in a small piece of cheesecloth, which is then known as a *sachet d'épices* (bag of spices), hereafter referred to as a sachet. By leaving a long tail of string on the sachet, you can tie one end to the handle of your soup pot. This makes it easier to find and remove the sachet when the spices have contributed the desired flavor to the soup. A large teaball can be used in place of cheese-cloth and string to make a sachet.

EQUIPMENT

Soup-making equipment is simple. Most of the soups in this book require just a single vessel for cooking the soup, though some do require the use of a second, usually smaller, vessel. You can make soup in just about any container large enough to accommodate the ingredients, so the recipes in this book simply call for a soup pot. Your soup pot should have a heavy bottom (to protect against scorching) and a capacity of about one gallon or more (most of the recipes yield two to three quarts). If, as in the French onion soup or shrimp bisque, the recipe calls for caramelizing or searing an ingredient before liquid is added, you should choose a pot with a wide bottom to expose more of that ingredient to direct heat than a narrow pot would. Otherwise, your soup pot should be taller than it is wide. This configuration results in less surface area, which means that less liquid will evaporate during cooking. It is best to avoid aluminum pots, particularly for cream soup, because the action of spoons and whisks against the pot can cause the soup to take on a grayish cast. Pots made of (or at least lined with) a nonreactive material, such as stainless steel, anodized aluminum, or enameled cast iron, are better choices.

For pureed and cream soups, you will need a strainer and equipment to do the pureeing. This can be a blender, hand-held blender, food processor, or food mill. A blender will give you the finest puree, followed by the food mill, food processor, and, fi-nally, the hand-held blender. If you use a blender or food processor, be sure the lid is se-curely closed before turning it on. An explosion of hot soup may cause severe burns, and

will definitely make you unhappy as you clean up your wasted soup. To be on the safe side, let the soup cool a bit before pureeing it.

Finally, you will also need a variety of small equipment: spoons and other stirring implements, tongs, a whisk, a ladle, measuring cups (for both liquid and dry ingredients), and measuring spoons. You might also need storage containers or bags for storing extra soup. And, of course, you will need something in which to serve the soup: a tureen and/or cups, bowls, soup plates, mugs, or crocks, depending on the soup.

COOKING

Most soups are cooked at a gentle simmer, just long enough to develop good flavor and body. Unless specifically instructed to do so, don't boil soups. An even simmer prevents scorching vegetables and thick soups at the bottom of the pot, and minimizes the rate of liquid evaporation. If a soup is accidentally allowed to boil and the liquid level drops dramatically, replace the amount lost with broth or water.

To preserve fresh flavors, cook ingredients only until tender. Add vegetables according to their cooking times. Add herbs and spices when the recipe instructs, unless you want to change the flavor of the soup. There is a direct relationship between the length of time the seasonings simmer and the quality and intensity of flavor they add. Fresh herbs lose flavor with long cooking times while spices become more intense. Wrapping herbs and spices in cheesecloth or a teaball to make a sachet allows you to remove them without straining the soup.

Stir soups from time to time to prevent starchy ingredients from sticking to the bottom of the pot. Throughout the cooking process, a shallow kitchen spoon or similar skimming uten-sil should be used to remove any scum or foam which forms on the surface so that the best flavor, texture, and appearance is obtained.

Taste a soup frequently and, when the flavor is fully developed and all of the ingredi-ents are tender, serve it right away or cool and store it as described below. Although some soups may develop a more rounded, mellow flavor if served the day after they are pre-pared, no soup benefits from hours on the stove. Not only will the flavor become dull and flat, but the nutritive value will also be greatly decreased.

ADJUSTING CONSISTENCY

Thick soups, especially those made with starchy vegetables or dried beans, may continue to thicken during cooking and storage. As a general rule, creams and bisques should be about as thick as cold heavy cream and liquid enough to pour from a ladle into a bowl. Purees should be somewhat thicker.

For a soup that has become too thick, add an appropriately flavored broth in small amounts until the proper consistency is reached. Check the seasoning before serving.

For a soup that is too thin, dissolve a small amount of cornstarch or arrowroot in a lit-tle broth or water to make a starch slurry. Add the slurry a little at a time to the simmering soup, stirring constantly. After each addition, let the soup simmer for a minute or two, so that you can assess the thickness. Keep adding the slurry gradually until the soup has reached its desired thickness.

ADJUSTING FLAVOR AND SEASONING

Soups should be seasoned throughout the cooking process. There are dozens of ways to adjust the flavor of a soup. Meat or poultry base (see page 12) may be added to bolster a weak broth; however, this will affect the clarity. Chopped fresh herbs, a few drops of lemon or lime juice, Tabasco sauce, Worcestershire sauce, or grated citrus zest may be added to brighten a soup's flavor. These items should be added a little at a time, and the seasoning carefully checked after each addition. Salt and pepper to taste should be added just prior to serving, when the soup is at the correct temperature.

Most soup recipes can be doubled or tripled to make extra quantities to refrigerate or freeze until needed. If you are planning to store a soup, prepare it just up to the point at which final adjustments are made—seasoning, finishing with cream, or adding garnishes. Make the final adjustments after you have reheated the soup, just before serving.

One of the leading causes of foodborne illness is the failure to properly cool foods. There is a specific temperature range, from 41 to 140°F, often referred to as the danger zone, which is particularly hospitable to a variety of illness-causing bacteria and viruses. In order to be certain that your soups remain wholesome and flavorful in the refrigerator over the course of several days, it is critical that you understand how to handle hot liquids in a way that will avoid the proliferation of harmful microbes.

In order to rapidly cool soups (or any other liquid) and speed their progression through the danger zone, the following procedures should be followed. First, transfer the hot soup to a clean container. The container selected should be metal, because it is a good heat conductor. Plastic is fine for storage, but is a poor choice for actually cooling the soup. Next, place the entire container in a cold-water bath, with enough water to come up to the level of the hot soup in the container. Adding ice to the water will also help to reduce the length of time it takes to cool the liquid.

If you cool the soup in a sink, you can use bricks or a rack to elevate the container so that cold water is able to circulate beneath it. Stirring the soup as it cools helps to speed the process, as well as to prevent anaerobic bacteria (which thrive in the absence of oxygen) from growing in the center of the container. The larger the batch, the longer the soup will take to cool, and the more important it is to take every possible step to accelerate the cooling.

Once the liquid has cooled to about 45°F, it is ready to be refrigerated or frozen. Depending on the ingredients, refrigerated soups will remain wholesome for three to five days. Frozen soups can be stored for four to five months. Label the storage container with the name of the contents and the date of preparation, so you can keep track of what you have and how long it's been there.

REHEATING

To reheat a clear broth or soup that has not been thickened with a starchy ingredient, bring it to a boil. Adjust the seasoning and add the garnish. If the garnish needs reheating, reduce the heat and simmer accordingly.

Thick soups like purees, creams, chowders, and bisques, need to be reheated gently. Place a thin layer of water or broth in a heavy-gauge pot, then add the soup. At first, reheat the soup slowly over low heat, stirring frequently, until it softens slightly. Then, increase the heat to medium and bring the soup just to a simmer. Continue to stir frequently as the soup heats. If a soup has already been finished with cream, sour cream, or a liaison (a mixture of eggs and cream), it is especially important that the soup not come all the way up to a boil or it may curdle. Once the soup is reheated, adjust the seasoning and consistency as needed, and add any garnishes just before serving.

In order to reheat individual portions of soup in a microwave oven, the soup must be placed in a microwave-safe bowl and covered. It should be heated about one minute at high power, then stirred to distribute the heat evenly. Repeat the process until the soup is very hot.

SERVING

There is a frequently repeated mantra in professional kitchens: Serve hot foods hot and cold foods cold. Accordingly, cold soups should be thoroughly chilled and served in chilled cups, bowls, or glasses. Hot soups should be served very hot in heated cups, bowls, mugs, crocks, or soup plates. The thinner the soup, the more important this is. Broth-style soups lose their heat rapidly, so they should be nearly at a boil before they are ladled into heated cups. Remember, the more surface area is exposed to air, the more quickly the soup will cool. This is one reason that broth-style soups are traditionally served in cups rather than the flatter, wider soup plates or bowls often used for cream soups and purees.

broths

AMONG A SOUP'S MOST IMPORTANT ELEMENTS is the liquid upon which it is built. A broth is at the heart of most of these soups. If they are prepared in large batches and frozen for later use, homemade broths can become a staple convenience food that eliminates the need for canned broth or bouillon cubes. In addition to the four basic broths in this chapter, you will find recipes to prepare a number of broth-style soups.

Broths are incredibly versatile. They can be garnished, served as is, or used as a base for a more elaborate soup. Rich, homemade broths may be served with whatever you have on hand in the refrigerator for a quick lunch or Sunday evening supper: a little chopped meat; some leftover cooked grains, vegetables, or beans; a splash of tomato juice; or a sprinkling of fresh herbs and a big crouton.

MAIN INGREDIENTS FOR BROTHS

Broths are a liquid essence of flavor, so the best broths are made from the most flavorful meats, fish, vegetables, and aromatics. Meat cuts should be from more exercised parts of the animal, such as the shank, neck, chuck, or bottom round. The more fully developed the muscle, the more pronounced the flavor. The same rule holds true for poultry. In this case, stewing hens or more mature game birds are the best choice. They have a deeper flavor than younger birds.

Fish should also be carefully selected. Freshness is of tremendous concern, as is the relative leanness or oiliness of the fish. Generally speaking, it is best to use lean, white-fleshed fish, such as sole, halibut, cod, or flounder. Richer, oilier fish, such as salmon and tuna, tend to lose their fresh flavor when their delicate oils are subjected to high temperatures for even short periods. Shellfish are generally cooked still in their shells in a small amount of liquid to produce excellent broths. The broth must then be strained very carefully to remove all traces of grit or sand.

Vegetable broths are made from any reasonable combination of vegetables. A selection of wholesome trimmings from a variety of vegetables can be combined to make a broth, or a specific recipe can be followed.

Whatever you select as the basis of your broth, look over the ingredients carefully. Remove any extra fat from birds or meats. Trim heavy stem or root ends from vegetables. Smell your ingredients. They should have a fresh, appetizing aroma and no hint of spoiling.

Most broths are started with the simplest of all liquids: cool, fresh water. In some cases you may elect to use a broth as the base liquid. This will produce what is sometimes referred to as a double broth.

Observe the following formulas to get a broth that is deep, complex, full-bodied, and flavorful. To produce 2 quarts broth, you will need:

- 4–5 pounds meat or poultry to 3 quarts cold water

- 5–6 pounds fish or shellfish to 3 quarts cold water

- 3–4 pounds vegetables to 3 quarts cold water

SUPPORTING FLAVORS

The point of making a broth is to produce a rich, flavorful liquid. To make a well-balanced, interesting broth, you can introduce the appropriate seasonings and flavorings, in the role of supporting flavors, as the broth simmers.

Vegetables combinations, herb or spice combinations, and wines can be included as supporting flavors. You can vary the time you add these ingredients, as well as the way in which they are prepared before they are added. This permits you to modify a basic broth formula to make a variety of broths, ranging from a traditional double-rich chicken broth to a Japanese-style miso broth.

For example, you can gently stew leeks, onions, mushrooms, and parsnips in a little oil to make a broth with a subtle color and flavor. Or, you can cook onions, carrots, celery, and a bit of tomato puree until browned to make a deeply colored and flavored broth.

As you taste your simmering broth, be conscious of these supporting flavors. If the herbs and spices are too strong, you can easily remove them if they were added as a sachet. It is more difficult to fish out little bits of carrot or celery, so use the recipes here as a starting point, before you decide to dramatically increase or decrease any specific ingredient.

A quick glance through this or any other cookbook will offer endless inspiration for garnishing broths. Simple items, such as herbs or finely diced vegetables, are traditional choices. Other options include diced or julienned meats, pieces of fish or shellfish, dumplings, noodles, rice, croutons, quenelles, and wontons.

Although there are strong arguments in favor of making your own broths, the fact remains that, in some situations, the most reasonable course of action is to use a commercially prepared broth or soup-base concentrate.

Full-strength broths are available in cans and aseptic packages. Some markets also sell frozen broth. Bases are available dehydrated (powdered or cubed bouillon) or as a highly concentrated paste. Not all broths and bases are created equal, however. Read the labels carefully. When buying broth, choose low-sodium, fat-free varieties when available. Avoid bases that rely on high-sodium ingredients for flavor. Quality broths and bases are made from meats, bones, vegetables, spices, and aromatics—the same ingredients you would use to make your own broth.

Whenever possible, test three or more brands. Prepare them according to the package instructions and taste each one. Judge the appropriateness of flavor, saltiness, balance, and depth.

Having decided that a broth or base meets your standards for quality, flavor, and cost, learn how to make any simple adjustments you find necessary. For example, you might sauté or roast more vegetables and simmer them in a diluted base, perhaps along with some aromatic herbs. A base can also be used to rescue a weak homemade broth. Adding a little base will deepen the flavor and improve the broth, and the base will be improved by the natural body of the homemade broth.

EVALUATING THE QUALITY OF BROTHS

The best broths are those which capture the full flavor of the main flavoring ingredients. A broth should be rich and aromatic. Broths should not feel like water on the tongue; they should have a discernible body. The color will vary by type, but will usually range from a pale gold to a deep amber.

If you use the appropriate ingredients and follow a good recipe, such as those included here, you will be rewarded with a rich, balanced, and aromatic broth. However, some problems can occur. Some common faults and the ways to avoid or correct them are discussed here:

- *Weak flavor.* If the proper ratio of flavoring ingredient to liquid has not been observed, the broth will have a weak taste. If you make a point of tasting the broth as it cooks, you will be able to add more of your major flavoring ingredient before it finishes simmering. Or, you can continue cooking the strained broth at a very gentle simmer to permit the broth to cook down, concentrating the flavor.

- *Flavor of supporting ingredients dominates.* The aromatics you include, such as vegetables, tomato puree, herbs, or spices, should act as grace notes, contributing only subtle flavors. A good safety net is to use a sachet or *bouquet garni* to add herbs or spices. Then, if the broth becomes unbalanced, you can easily pull out the sachet or bouquet. If a particular vegetable, such as celery or carrot, dominates, you may be able to compensate by adding other ingredients as a counterbalance. A broth that tastes unbalanced on its own can sometimes be the perfect foundation for another soup. Another option is to strain the broth and simmer it with a bit more of the major flavoring ingredient. Remember to record your observations about the broth, and note how you might correct the problem when you make it next time.

- *Cloudy broth.* If your broth boils, rather than simmers, it might be cloudy after straining. A cloudy broth may be perfectly fine for a thick vegetable, puree, or cream soup. However, if you meant to make a very clear broth, you can clarify it using one of the techniques described in the accompanying sidebar on consommé.

- *Sour, off, or musty flavor.* Assuming that your ingredients were fresh and wholesome, your broth may still develop an unpleasant flavor or aroma for one of the following reasons: The soup was allowed to boil. It was not properly skimmed during preparation. It was cooled and/or stored improperly. Use all your senses—sight, hearing, smell, taste—to monitor the broth as it cooks, to alert you to problems before they have gone too far to correct easily.

basic broth method

➤ *Combine the major flavoring ingredients with cool liquid and bring gently to a simmer.*

It is important to begin with cool liquid (fig. 1). Starting with hot liquid will cause proteins in the meat to coagulate and starches in the vegetables to gelatinize too quickly, which impedes flavor extraction. Beginning with cool liquid will gently extract as much flavor as possible as the liquid slowly heats. And, in the case of meat-based broths, it will help establish a natural clarification process. A hard boil should always be avoided, because it could cook out the flavor of the ingredients. Furthermore, a vigorous boiling action will cause fat and impurities to be mixed back into the broth, clouding the mixture. A gentle simmer will cause these elements to collect on the surface where they can be skimmed away.

➤ *Skim.*

As the broth comes to a simmer, be sure to skim the surface carefully to remove as much foam and fat as possible (fig. 2). If allowed to remain in the pot, these elements will eventually cloud the broth, and could cause an unpleasant aroma or taste. The most foam is thrown in the first hour or so of cooking time, but you should skim the broth frequently throughout.

➤ *Add any remaining ingredients at appropriate intervals.*

Some vegetables and herbs will release the best flavor into a broth quickly. Continued cooking, rather than intensifying the flavor, could actually cook away the delicate, volatile oils that hold their flavor essence. Most recipes will indicate which items to add later in the cooking process. The rule of thumb is that the denser the ingredient, the earlier it is added (fig. 3).

➤ *Simmer until the flavor, color, and body are fully developed.*

The only way to be sure that your broth is developing properly is to taste it from time to time, which allows you the opportunity to make corrections if necessary. At first, there will not be much flavor at all, although a broth will often develop a

4.

rich smell very quickly. Both the flavor and aroma should intensify as the broth cooks. As the broth begins to simmer, it will look cloudy and may be full of particles. After the first hour or so, and several careful skimmings, the broth should be much clearer and start to take on a distinct golden color (fig. 4).

Final seasoning and flavor adjustments are generally done after the major ingredients have given up their maximum flavor. Meats and poultry used to prepare broths can be removed from the simmering broth when they are fully cooked and tender. The meat can be pulled away from the bone and used to garnish the finished broth, or it can be saved for another use. If the meat is completely cooked, but the broth is not as flavorful as you wish, pull the meat from the bones, and return the bones to the pot. Continue simmering until the broth is finished.

Generally speaking, broths are properly cooked at about the following times:

5.

- Meat: 4–6 hours
- Poultry: 2–3 hours
- Fish: 30–45 minutes
- Vegetables: 30 minutes to 1 hour (The type of vegetables used will determine the cooking time; overcooking vegetable broth results in bitter, acidic flavors.)

6.

 Strain.

Allow the broth to cool slightly before straining. Professional chefs use a large cone-shaped sieve to strain broth but, in many home kitchens, the most commonly available straining equipment is a colander and/or a fine-mesh sieve. Set the colander over a clean metal container, such as a second soup pot. Use extreme care when straining hot liquids to avoid burning yourself; try to disturb the solid ingredients as little as possible or the broth could become excessively cloudy. Use a ladle to transfer as much broth as possible to the colander (fig. 5), then gently pour the remaining broth and solids into the colander. For extra clarity, strain the broth a second time through a sieve. The broth is now ready to be garnished (fig. 6) and served or cooled and stored following the procedures outlined in chapter 1.

Note: A tall pot with a pasta insert is particularly useful for making broth. The pasta insert allows you to lift the solids out of the broth instead of straining the broth through a colander. You can then strain the broth through a fine-mesh sieve if you like.

chicken broth

Chicken broth is a crucial ingredient in soup making, and the flavor of homemade is hard to beat. You can double, or even quadruple, this recipe and freeze the extra so that you always have some on hand. If you freeze the broth in ice-cube trays, then transfer the cubes to freezer bags, it's easy to thaw exactly the amount you need. If you're short on time and must use canned broth, choose the all-natural or fat-free, reduced-sodium varieties.

MAKES ABOUT 2 QUARTS

4 pounds stewing hen or chicken parts or meaty bones, such as backs and necks

3 quarts cold water

1 large onion, diced (about 1¼ cups)

1 carrot, diced (about ⅓ cup)

1 celery stalk, diced (about ½ cup)

5–6 whole black peppercorns

3–4 parsley stems

1 bay leaf

1 sprig fresh thyme

1½ teaspoons salt, or to taste

Place the chicken and water in a large pot (the water should cover the chicken by at least 2 inches; add more if necessary). Bring the water slowly to a boil over medium heat.

As the water comes to a boil, skim any foam that rises to the surface. Adjust the heat once a boil is reached, so that a slow, lazy simmer is established. Cover partially, and simmer 2 hours, skimming as often as necessary.

Add the remaining ingredients. Continue to simmer, skimming the surface as necessary, until the broth is fully flavored, about 1 hour.

If using hen or chicken parts, remove them and cool slightly. Dice or shred the meat, and reserve to garnish the broth or save for another use. Discard the skin and bones.

Strain the broth through a fine sieve or cheesecloth-lined colander into a large metal container. Discard the solids.

If you are using the broth right away, skim off any fat on the surface. If you are not using the broth right away, cool it quickly by transferring it to a metal container (if it's not in one already) and placing the container in a sink filled with ice-cold water. Stir the broth as it cools, and then transfer it to storage containers. Store in the refrigerator, up to 5 days, or in the freezer, up to 3 months. Label and date the containers clearly before putting them into the freezer.

To make a double chicken broth, use cold chicken broth instead of water.

Some stores sell packages of necks and backs that can be used to prepare broth. This broth can also be made with the carcasses of roasted birds. Save the bones after all of the meat has been pulled or carved away (freeze them if you will not be making the broth within a day or two). You will need the carcasses of about 3 birds.

If the broth is allowed to chill in the refrigerator overnight, the fat will rise to the surface and harden. It is then easy to lift away. The broth will then be completely fat free, and will only have the salt that you have chosen to add.

If, after straining the broth, you find the flavor to be weaker than you would like, simply put the broth back on the stove and boil it down until the flavor has concentrated.

beef broth

For the clearest broth, be sure to skim frequently as it comes to a simmer, and as often as necessary thereafter. Never let it reach a boil; this will make the broth cloudy. In describing the proper state of a broth as it simmers, the French use the verb fremir—*to tremble. This means that there should be movement on the surface, but only a few lazy bubbles should actually be seen breaking the surface.*

MAKES ABOUT 2 QUARTS

4 pounds beef (chuck, ribs, shank, or neck)

3 quarts water

1½ medium onions, coarsely chopped (about 2 cups)

1 leek, white and light green part, coarsely chopped (about 1¼ cups)

1 carrot, coarsely chopped (about ⅓ cup)

1 celery stalk, coarsely chopped (about ½ cup)

¼ cup celery leaves

3–4 parsley stems

3–4 black peppercorns

1 bay leaf

2 teaspoons salt, or to taste

½ teaspoon dried or 1 sprig fresh thyme

Preheat the oven to 400°F.

Put the beef in a roasting pan and place in the oven. Roast until deep brown, 45 minutes to 1 hour.

Transfer the beef to a soup pot. Pour 1 cup water into the hot roasting pan and scrape the bottom to loosen any drippings; pour over the beef. Add the remaining water (there should be enough to cover the beef by 2 inches; add more water if necessary) and bring to a simmer. Cover partially and simmer gently, 2 hours. Skim frequently any scum that rises to the surface.

Add the remaining ingredients. Continue to simmer gently until the broth has developed a full, rich flavor, about 2 hours. Remove the meat and reserve to garnish the broth or save for another use.

Strain the broth through a fine sieve or cheesecloth-lined colander into a large metal container. Discard the solids.

If you are using the broth right away, skim off any fat on the surface. If you are not using the broth immediately, cool it quickly by placing the container in a sink filled with ice-cold water. Stir the broth as it cools, and then transfer it to storage containers. Store in the refrigerator, up to 5 days, or in the freezer, up to 3 months. Label and date the containers clearly before putting them into the freezer. Remove any fat that has hardened on the surface before reheating.

fish broth

Use only the bones from mild, lean white fish, such as halibut or sole, to make this broth. Bones from oily fish, like salmon, will make a broth that is overpowering. The bones must be perfectly fresh. If you won't be able to prepare it right away, store the bones in the freezer. Shells from shrimp, crab, and lobsters can be substituted for the bones to prepare a crustacean broth. They can be stored in the freezer, too, until you have enough ingredients and time to make a batch. This recipe, as well as those for other broths, can easily be multiplied if you have a good quantity of ingredients on hand. It takes no longer to simmer a gallon of broth than it does two quarts. You can freeze any that you don't plan to use right away. Frozen homemade broth is a convenience food that can help make meal preparation a snap on busy nights.

MAKES ABOUT 2 QUARTS

2 tablespoons vegetable oil

5 pounds fish bones from lean, white fish

2 onions, thinly sliced (about 2¹/₂ cups)

2 leeks, white and light green parts, thinly sliced (about 2¹/₂ cups)

2 celery stalks, thinly sliced (about 1 cup)

1 cup white mushrooms or mushroom stems, thinly sliced, optional

1 cup dry white wine, optional

2¹/₂ quarts cold water

10 black peppercorns

6 parsley stems

2 sprigs fresh thyme, tarragon, or dill

2 bay leaves

Heat the oil in a soup pot over low heat. Add the fish bones, onions, leeks, celery, and mushrooms, if using. Stir until all the ingredients are evenly coated with oil. Cover the pot and cook, without stirring, about 5 minutes.

Add the wine, if using, and simmer until the wine is reduced by half. Add the water, peppercorns, parsley stems, fresh herbs, and bay leaves. Bring the broth just up to a simmer. Continue to simmer gently, 35–45 minutes.

Strain the broth through a fine sieve or cheesecloth-lined colander. Discard the solids. If the broth is not to be used right away, cool it thoroughly before storing it in the refrigerator, up to 3 days, or in the freezer, up to 6 weeks. Label and date the containers clearly before putting them into the freezer.

vegetable broth

The light flavor of this vegetable broth is far superior to that of commercially prepared vegetable broths, which always seem to taste like the can they came in. In addition to its role in making soup, vegetable broth can be used to prepare grain or bean dishes, instead of water or chicken broth. It is also good as the cooking liquid for pan-steamed vegetables. The vegetables listed here should be thought of as suggestions. Feel free to use other vegetables, as long as they will not give the finished broth a strong odor or color (for instance, beets and beet greens might not be appropriate). Starchy vegetables may make the broth foam over as it simmers. Beyond that, let your own taste be your guide.

MAKES ABOUT 2 QUARTS

2 teaspoons olive or corn oil

1–2 garlic cloves, finely minced

2 teaspoons minced shallots

3 quarts water

1 large onion, thinly sliced (about 1¼ cups)

1 leek, white, light green, and dark green parts, trimmed and sliced (about 3 cups)

1 celery stalk, thinly sliced (about ½ cup)

1 carrot, thinly sliced (about ⅓ cup)

1 parsnip, thinly sliced (about ⅓ cup)

1 cup thinly sliced broccoli stems

1 cup thinly sliced fennel, with some tops

½ cup dry white wine or vermouth, optional

1 tablespoon salt or to taste

4–5 whole black peppercorns

½ teaspoon juniper berries

1 bay leaf

1 sprig fresh or ¼ teaspoon dried thyme

Heat the oil in a soup pot over medium heat. Add the garlic and shallots and cook, stirring frequently, until they are translucent, 3–4 minutes.

Add the remaining ingredients and bring slowly to a simmer. Cook until the broth has a good flavor, about 1 hour.

Strain the broth through a sieve. Allow it to cool completely before storing in the refrigerator.

This broth can be prepared in large batches, then frozen for later use. Be sure to label and date the containers so that you use the oldest broth first. Freeze the broth in ice cube trays, then store the frozen cubes in large freezer bags so you can thaw exactly the amount needed at any given time.

When preparing vegetables for other dishes, save any wholesome trim or peels that you want to put into the broth. Then every few days, put on a pot of broth. You will get a nutrient boost, as well as avoiding the use of canned broths that might be higher in sodium that you'd like.

consommé

Consommé is a strong, perfectly clear broth of the best quality, enriched by simmering it gently with a combination of lean ground meat (beef, chicken, or fish, for example), egg whites, aromatic vegetables, herbs and spices, and an acidic ingredient (such as tomatoes, wine, or lemon juice). As a further boost to both flavor and color, an oignon brûlé *(a halved onion that has been charred in a cast iron skillet, on a griddle, or directly over a gas flame) is often added. These ingredients are mixed evenly to make what professional chefs refer to as a* clarification. *For the best results, the broth and the clarification should be thoroughly chilled.*

MAKES ABOUT 2 QUARTS

3 quarts cold broth

1¹/₂ pounds lean ground meat (use chicken breast with chicken broth, beef with beef broth, etc.)

5 lightly beaten egg whites

¹/₄ cup tomato puree

¹/₂ onion, charred if desired, finely diced

1 carrot, finely diced (about ¹/₃ cup)

1 celery stalk, finely diced (about ¹/₂ cup)

Thoroughly blend the cold broth with the other ingredients. Place the mixture over moderate heat and stir almost constantly. As the broth heats, the meat and egg-white proteins will coagulate and rise to the surface, forming what is known as a *raft*. Once the raft begins to form, stop stirring. Adjust the heat to maintain a very gently simmer. After the raft is completely formed, break a small hole in it. This lets the steam escape, and allows you to see how fast the consommé is cooking. Many small bubbles should be rising to the surface, but it should not be at a full boil.

Taste the consommé to determine when it is fully flavored. Consommés generally reach a flavor peak after simmering for 1–1¹/₂ hours. The raft usually will not start to sink or break apart before then, unless it is cooking either too quickly or too slowly. Some chefs suggest that you baste the raft occasionally to get the best flavor extraction and to prevent the raft from breaking up too soon.

Once the consommé is properly cooked, enlarge the hole in the raft so that you can fit a ladle through it easily. Ladle the consommé through a coffee filter- or cheesecloth-lined strainer. It is important to disturb the raft as little as possible, to avoid clouding the consommé.

Your finished consommé should be crystal clear, highly flavored, richly colored, and full bodied. It should also be completely fat free. If time allows, chill the consommé and remove the fat that solidifies on the surface. If not, drag strips of paper towel across the surface to pick up any droplets of fat. Many of the garnishes used for broths can also be used for consommés. Choose garnishes that won't cloud the consommé, cook them separately if necessary, and add them to individual portions just before serving.

roast turkey broth with caramelized butternut squash and sage dumplings

This double broth is perfect for a cold winter's day. If you happen to have the carcass of a roast turkey on hand, chop it into large pieces and roast it instead of using fresh bones. You can also add leftover roast turkey meat to the soup. If you are not serving all the soup at once, refrigerate the broth, squash, and dumplings separately, and reheat only as much as you need.

MAKES 8 SERVINGS

4 pounds turkey legs or meaty turkey bones (wings, backs, and necks) and giblets (excluding the liver)

3 quarts Chicken Broth (page 16), or as needed

1 large onion, thinly sliced (about 1¼ cups)

1 carrot, thinly sliced (about ⅓ cup)

1 celery stalk, thinly sliced (about ½ cup)

5–6 whole black peppercorns

3–4 parsley stems

1 bay leaf

1 sprig fresh thyme

Salt, to taste

2 tablespoons unsalted butter

2 cups diced butternut squash (about 1 pound)

Freshly ground white pepper, to taste

1 recipe Sage Dumplings (page 197)

Preheat the oven to 400°F. Spread the turkey legs or bones in a single layer in a roasting pan. Roast until deep golden brown, about 1 hour.

Transfer the turkey legs or bones to a large soup pot. Add 2 cups of the broth to the hot roasting pan and scrape the bottom of the pan with a wooden spoon to loosen any drippings. Pour over the turkey legs or bones.

Add enough broth to cover by at least 2 inches. Bring slowly to a boil over medium heat. As the liquid comes to a boil, skim any foam that rises to the surface. Adjust the heat once a boil is reached, so that a slow, lazy simmer is established. Simmer 1 hour, skimming as necessary.

Add the onion, carrot, celery, peppercorns, parsley stems, bay leaf, thyme, and salt. Continue to simmer, skimming the surface as necessary, until broth is fully flavored, about 1 hour.

While the broth is simmering, heat the butter in a large ovenproof skillet over medium heat. Add the squash and cook, stirring occasionally, until brown on all sides, 15–20 minutes. Season the squash with salt and pepper and place the skillet in the preheated oven. Roast the squash until tender, about 10 minutes. Remove the squash from the oven, drain off any excess fat, and set aside.

When the broth is fully flavored, strain it through a fine sieve or cheese-cloth-lined colander into a clean soup pot. If you used turkey legs, remove the skin, pull the meat from the bones, dice, and return it to the broth, or save for another purpose. Discard the remaining solids.

Add the squash and the dumplings to the broth. Return to a simmer briefly to heat through. Season with salt and pepper. Serve in heated bowls.

stracciatella

The name of this simple soup means "rags." By whipping the soup as you add beaten eggs and Parmesan cheese, the eggs cook into threads, or rags. Use either homemade or quality canned broth to prepare this soup.

MAKES 6 TO 8 SERVINGS

6 cups Chicken or Beef Broth (pages 16, 18)

2 whole eggs

¼ cup freshly grated Parmesan cheese

Salt, to taste

Freshly ground white pepper, to taste

6–8 slices Italian bread

Extra-virgin olive oil, as needed

1 garlic clove, halved

1 tablespoon chopped parsley, optional

Preheat the oven to 375°F. Bring the broth to a simmer in a soup pot.

Whisk the eggs and cheese together in a small bowl. Whisk the broth constantly as you add the egg mixture to broth in a thin stream. Season soup with salt and pepper. Keep warm.

Brush each slice of bread with olive oil and rub with the cut side of the garlic clove. Place on a baking sheet, and toast in the oven until lightly browned and crisp, 4–5 minutes.

Place each piece of toast in the bottom of a heated soup bowl and ladle the soup over the toast. Sprinkle with parsley, if using, and serve immediately.

avgolemono (greek egg and lemon soup)

Avgolemono is the name of a soup and a sauce. Both are made with chicken broth, eggs, and lemon. The differences between the two are that the sauce is thicker than the soup, and the soup contains rice. The soup should have a definite taste of lemon, but not an overpowering one. Use only freshly squeezed lemon juice for a clean, delicate flavor.

MAKES 6 TO 8 SERVINGS

6 cups Chicken Broth (page 16)

$1/_3$ cup long-grain white rice

4 eggs, separated

Salt, to taste

Freshly ground white pepper, to taste

Freshly squeezed lemon juice, to taste

Bring the broth to a simmer in a soup pot. Add the rice and cook until tender, about 15 minutes.

Whip the egg yolks in a large bowl until thickened. Whip the egg whites in another bowl to soft peaks. Fold the whites into the yolks. Add the egg mixture to the simmering broth, whipping constantly. The soup will become frothy and thick.

Season the soup with salt, pepper, and lemon juice. Serve in heated bowls.

petite marmite

Though named and claimed by the French, this heavenly broth full of meat, poultry, and vegetables can be found in one form or another in virtually every world cuisine. Some serve the broth as a first course with the meats and vegetables following; others present the meats and vegetables as the soup's garnish (the approach suggested here). Add some crusty bread and, either way you serve it, this soup makes a healthy and hearty meal.

MAKES 8 SERVINGS

1 chicken (about 3 pounds)

1½ pounds beef bottom round

3 quarts Chicken Broth, cold (page 16)

2 celery stalks, diced (about 1 cup)

2 leeks, white and light green parts, diced (about 2 cups)

1 large onion, diced (about 1½ cups)

1 large carrot, diced (about ½ cup)

1 large white turnip, diced (about 1 cup)

¼ head white or green cabbage, diced or shredded (about 2 cups)

Sachet: 1 bay leaf, ¼ teaspoon dried thyme, 4 black peppercorns, 4 parsley stems, and 1 peeled garlic clove enclosed in a large teaball or tied in a cheesecloth pouch

Salt, to taste

Freshly ground black pepper, to taste

¼ cup chopped parsley

1½ cups Croutons (page 183)

Remove the neck and giblets from the cavity of the chicken. Rinse the cavity with cold water. Place the beef and chicken in a large soup pot and cover with cold broth. Bring to a simmer over low heat. With a shallow, flat spoon, skim the scum as it rises to the surface and discard. Simmer until the beef and chicken are fork-tender, about 2 hours.

Remove the beef and chicken and cool. Strain the broth through a fine sieve or cheesecloth-lined colander. Return the broth to the soup pot.

Add the celery, leeks, onion, carrot, turnip, cabbage, and sachet to the broth. Bring to a simmer and cook until the vegetables are tender, 15–20 minutes. Remove the sachet and discard.

When the beef and chicken have cooled, remove any gristle from the beef and dice the meat. Remove the skin and bones from the chicken. Dice the chicken meat. Return the diced beef and chicken to the broth. Simmer 5 minutes to heat thoroughly. Season with salt and pepper.

Serve in heated bowls, garnished with parsley and croutons.

Some people do not consider a petite marmite to be authentic unless it contains diced marrow. To add the marrow, first soak 1 pound marrow bones in cold water for several hours; rinse well. Place the bones in a pot, cover with cold water, and bring to a simmer. Cook until the marrow can easily be scooped out of the bone with a spoon, 45 minutes to 1 hour. Dice the marrow and add it to the broth when you add the diced meat and poultry.

You may also substitute any of the following meats for, or combine them with, the beef and chicken: venison or other game meats, oxtails, pheasant or other game birds, turkey, ham hocks, pork, or lamb. The total weight should be about 4 pounds. Increase the broth as needed to cover the meats completely and follow the method appropriately.

french onion soup

The secret to making a fine French onion soup is to give it lots of time to develop flavor. The onions should be cooked slowly, until they become deeply caramelized. Then, they should be simmered in broth for nearly an hour to allow their flavors to permeate the broth. If you have the time, we recommend you make the soup the day before you serve it to allow the flavor to mature and mellow. Taking this route will also give you the opportunity to lift away any excess fat that has solidified on the surface.

MAKES 8 SERVINGS

¼ cup olive or vegetable oil

4 medium onions, thinly sliced (about 5 cups)

2 garlic cloves, minced (about 1 teaspoon)

½ cup brandy

1½ quarts Chicken or Beef Broth, heated
(pages 16, 18)

Sachet: 3 to 4 parsley stems, ½ teaspoon each
dried thyme and tarragon, and 1 bay leaf enclosed
in a large teaball or tied in a cheesecloth pouch

Salt, to taste

Freshly ground black pepper, to taste

8 slices French bread

1 cup grated Gruyère cheese, or as needed

Heat the oil in a soup pot over medium-low heat. Add the onions and cook without stirring until the onions begin to brown on the bottom. Raise the heat to medium, stir, and continue to cook, stirring occasionally, until the onions are deeply caramelized (dark golden brown). The total cooking time will be 30–45 minutes. If the onions begin to scorch, add a few tablespoons of water and continue cooking.

Add the garlic and continue to cook an additional minute. Add the brandy and simmer until the liquid has nearly evaporated, 2–3 minutes.

Add the broth and sachet. Bring to a simmer and cook, partially covered, for 45 minutes to 1 hour, skimming the surface as necessary and discarding any fat. Remove the sachet and discard. Season with salt and pepper.

When ready to serve, preheat the oven to 350°F and bring 2 quarts water to a boil. Ladle the soup into individual ovenproof soup crocks. Top each crock with a slice of bread and sprinkle with grated cheese, covering the bread completely, and allowing the cheese to touch the edge of the crock.

Set the soup crocks in a baking dish and add enough boiling water to reach ⅔ up the sides of the crocks. Bake until the soup is thoroughly heated and the cheese is lightly browned, 10–15 minutes. Serve immediately.

clear vegetable soup

This soup bursts with the flavor of fresh vegetables. Serve it with Cheddar Rusks (page 184) if you like, and feel free to experiment with different combinations of vegetables.

MAKES 8 SERVINGS

3 tablespoons olive oil

2 carrots, diced (about ²/₃ cup)

1 onion, diced (about 1¹/₄ cups)

1 celery stalk, diced (about ¹/₂ cup)

¹/₃ cup diced turnip

¹/₂ leek, diced (about ³/₄ cup)

¹/₂ cup diced shredded cabbage

2 quarts Vegetable Broth (page 20)

Sachet: 5 black peppercorns, 5 parsley stems, 1 bay leaf, and 1 fresh sprig or ¹/₂ teaspoon dried thyme enclosed in a large teaball or tied in a cheesecloth pouch

2 plum tomatoes, peeled, seeded, and diced (page 36, about ¹/₂ cup)

¹/₂ cup peeled, diced yellow or white potato

¹/₂ cup fresh or frozen lima beans

¹/₂ cup fresh or frozen corn kernels

¹/₄ cup chopped flat-leaf parsley

Salt, to taste

Heat the oil in a soup pot over medium heat. Add the carrots, onion, celery, turnip, leek, and cabbage, and cook until softened, 10–15 minutes.

Add the broth and sachet. Bring to a simmer and cook, 10 minutes.

Add the tomatoes, potatoes, lima beans, corn, and parsley. Continue to simmer until the potatoes are tender, 10–15 minutes.

Remove the sachet and discard. Season with salt. Serve in heated bowls.

amish-style chicken and corn soup

The Amish are famous for their use of herbs and spices. The saffron in this soup lends it a deep golden color as well as a subtle flavor. If you prefer, the soup can be prepared without the saffron, however.

MAKES 8 SERVINGS

½ stewing hen or fowl, quartered

2 quarts Chicken Broth (page 16)

¾ cup chopped onion

½ cup chopped carrot

½ cup chopped celery

1 teaspoon crushed saffron threads

1 cup cooked egg noodles

¾ cup corn kernels (fresh or frozen)

½ cup finely diced celery

1 tablespoon chopped fresh flat-leaf parsley

Salt, to taste

Freshly ground black pepper, to taste

Combine the stewing hen with the broth, onions, carrots, celery, and saffron threads in a soup pot. Bring to a simmer and cook, about 1 hour, skimming the surface as necessary.

Remove the stewing hen from the broth. When cool enough to handle, pick the meat from the bones and cut into a neat dice.

Strain the saffron broth through a fine sieve.

Add the noodles, corn, and celery to the broth. Return the soup to a simmer. Season with the parsley, salt, and pepper. Serve in heated bowls.

about stewing hens

Stewing hens (or fowls) are the best choice for soups. They are more full-flavored than fryers or broilers, and you will end up with a soup that has a wonderfully rich flavor and body. You can use the entire bird to prepare a gallon of broth, then freeze the broth and cooked meat you won't need for this recipe separately, to be used as the basis for future soups. Just double the amount of water and chopped onion, carrot, and celery, omitting the saffron.

FACING PAGE: Adding aromatic vegetables (top left); adding freshly chopped parsley (top right); adding the corn before simmering (bottom left); checking the tenderness of the noodles (bottom right)

double chicken broth with shiitakes, scallions, and tofu

This soup is quick to prepare and makes a good introduction to a meal of stir-fried shrimp and vegetables. Double broth means simply that chicken broth is used to poach more chicken, which doubles the flavor of the broth. To serve this soup on its own as an entire meal, increase the amount of chicken breast and include as many of the following items as you like: broccoli florets, sliced celery, shredded bok choy or celery, cabbage, snow peas, green beans, chick peas, or cucumbers. Conclude the meal with a fruit sorbet or ice.

MAKES 8 SERVINGS

1 cup diced soft tofu

½ pound boneless, skinless chicken breast

2 quarts Chicken Broth (page 16)

8 shiitake mushrooms (dry or fresh)

6 scallions, sliced diagonally

2 tablespoons chopped fresh cilantro

2 teaspoons minced fresh ginger root

4 teaspoons soy or tamari sauce

½ teaspoon freshly ground black pepper, or to taste

Freshly squeezed lime juice, to taste

Place the tofu on paper toweling and let drain.

Trim any visible fat from the chicken breast and discard. Cut the chicken into strips.

Bring the broth to a simmer in a soup pot over high heat. Add the chicken, reduce the heat to low, and simmer, 10 minutes. Skim any foam that rises to the surface.

Add the tofu, shiitakes, scallions, cilantro, and ginger. Simmer until all the ingredients are heated through and the flavors are blended, 5–10 minutes.

Add the soy sauce, pepper, and lime juice. Serve in heated bowls.

chicken vegetable soup azteca

Once an important food for the Aztec and Maya peoples of Central America, chayote *is a pear-shaped fruit with furrowed, pale-green skin. It is also known as a* mirliton, *a* christophene, *and a* vegetable pear. *It has a rather mild flavor that has been described as a blend of cucumber, zucchini, and kohlrabi. The Bean and Cheese Rusks on page 185 complement this soup nicely.*

MAKES 8 SERVINGS

1 chayote

3 tablespoons olive oil, divided

1 poblano chile

2 garlic cloves, minced (about 1 teaspoon)

1 jalapeño pepper, minced (about 2 tablespoons)

1 teaspoon ground coriander
(preferably freshly ground)

1¹/₂ boneless, skinless chicken breasts,
cut into small cubes

1¹/₂ quarts Chicken Broth (page 16)

5 canned Italian plum tomatoes, chopped

1 small onion, diced (about 1 cup)

1 carrot, finely diced (about ¹/₃ cup)

1 celery stalk, finely diced (about ¹/₂ cup)

1 small yellow squash, finely diced (about 1 cup)

1 tablespoon chopped cilantro

Salt, to taste

Freshly ground black pepper, to taste

Preheat the oven to 350°F. Rub the chayote with 1 teaspoon of the oil and place on a baking sheet. Roast the chayote in the oven until the skin browns lightly and the flesh is barely tender, 25–30 minutes. When cool enough to handle, use a paring knife to scrape away the skin. Cut the chayote in half from top to bottom and use a spoon to scoop out the edible seed, which you can either discard or eat as a snack. Dice the flesh and set aside.

Increase the oven temperature to broil. Brush the poblano with 1 teaspoon of the oil. Place the poblano under the broiler and turn it as it roasts so that it blackens evenly on all sides. Put the poblano in a small bowl and cover, letting it steam for 10 minutes, then remove it from the bowl and pull off the skin. Use the back of a knife to scrape away any bits that don't come away easily. Remove and discard the seeds, ribs, and stem. Dice the flesh and set aside.

Heat the remaining oil in a soup pot over medium heat. Add the garlic, jalapeño pepper, and coriander. Cook, stirring, until slightly softened, about 4 minutes.

Add the chicken and cook, stirring occasionally, until the chicken is just cooked through, about 8 minutes.

Add the chayote, poblano, broth, tomatoes, onion, carrot, and yellow squash. Bring to a simmer and cook until all the vegetables are tender, about 30 minutes.

Add the cilantro and season with salt and pepper. Serve in heated bowls.

zucchini soup with cheddar rusks

When zucchini become large, their seeds can become a little bitter. If you have a giant-sized squash, halve it from blossom to stem end, scoop out the seeds with a tablespoon, then dice the remaining flesh. Smaller zucchini can be used seeds and all. The bacon provides a great deal of flavor to this soup, but if you prefer a vegetarian version, add a spoonful of minced sun-dried tomatoes along with the basil. Replace the bacon itself with a tablespoon or two of olive oil.

MAKES 8 SERVINGS

4 bacon strips, minced

2 onions, diced (about 2¹/₂ cups)

4 garlic cloves, minced (about 2 teaspoons)

4 medium zucchini, diced (7–8 cups)

6 cups Chicken Broth (page 16)

4 plum tomatoes, peeled, seeded, and chopped (page 26, about 1 cup)

¹/₂ cup tomato puree

4 tablespoons tarragon or cider vinegar

2 tablespoons minced fresh basil

¹/₂ teaspoon salt, or to taste

¹/₄ teaspoon freshly ground black pepper, or to taste

8 Cheddar Rusks (page 184)

Cook the bacon in a soup pot over medium heat until the fat is released and the bacon bits are crisp, 6–8 minutes.

Add the onions and garlic. Cook, stirring frequently, until the onions are a light golden brown, 8–10 minutes.

Add the zucchini, cover the pot, and cook until the zucchini starts to become translucent, about 5 minutes.

Add the broth, tomatoes, tomato puree, and vinegar. Bring the soup to a simmer and cook until the vegetables are very tender and the soup has developed a good flavor, 15–20 minutes.

Add the basil to the soup, and season with salt and pepper. Serve in heated bowls, garnished with cheddar rusks.

tomato and sweet pepper soup

When peppers and tomatoes begin to ripen in the late summer and fall, this soup is a delicious way to showcase their wonderful flavors. You can use a combination of red, green, and yellow peppers and tomatoes for an interesting appearance. You can also make this soup at other times of the year by substituting 2 cups drained, canned tomatoes for the fresh ones. To make this soup a little more elegant, serve with Goat Cheese Rusks (page 184). You might also omit the poppy-seed whipped cream and garnish with a spoonful of Pistou (page 200) instead.

MAKES 8 SERVINGS

¼ cup olive oil

1 onion, finely diced (about 1¼ cups)

2 garlic cloves, minced (about 1 teaspoon)

3 ripe tomatoes, peeled, seeded, and chopped (about 3 cups)

2 sweet red bell peppers, seeds and ribs removed, cut into thin strips (about 2 cups)

2 celery stalks, thinly sliced (about 1 cup)

6 cups Chicken Broth (page 16)

½ cup heavy cream

1 tablespoon poppy seeds, lightly crushed

½ teaspoon salt, or to taste

¼ teaspoon freshly ground white pepper, or to taste

Heat the oil in a soup pot over medium heat. Add the onion and garlic and stir to coat evenly with oil. Reduce the heat to low, cover the pot, and cook, 6–8 minutes.

Add the tomatoes, peppers, and celery to the pot, replace the cover, and continue to cook until the vegetables are tender and heated through, 6–8 minutes.

Add the broth. Bring to a simmer and cook, 20 minutes. Skim as needed.

Meanwhile, whip the cream until it forms soft peaks. Fold in the poppy seeds.

Season the soup with salt and pepper. Serve in heated bowls, topped with the poppy-seed whipped cream.

to peel fresh tomatoes

Bring a pot of water to a rolling boil. Score an X in the bottom of the tomatoes with a paring knife, then drop them into the boiling water, 15–30 seconds. Remove with a slotted spoon and place briefly in a bowl of ice water to cool. Peel away skin with paring knife, cut tomato in half, and remove seeds.

soto ayam
(indonesian chicken, noodle, and potato soup)

Don't let the long list of ingredients and steps deter you from making this soup. It's truly delicious and not all that much trouble to make, despite appearances. Any of the ingredients you can't find at your supermarket are available at Asian groceries. To crush the aromatic ingredients, cover with a piece of plastic wrap and smash with the bottom of a heavy pot or skillet.

MAKES 8 SERVINGS

1 small chicken (about 3 pounds)

2 teaspoons salt, divided

$^1/_2$ tablespoon vegetable oil

4 shallots, chopped

2 stalks fresh lemongrass, bottom 4 or 5 inches only, crushed

1 garlic clove, crushed

1-inch slice fresh ginger root, crushed

$^1/_2$ teaspoon crushed black peppercorns

$^1/_4$ teaspoon turmeric

$1^1/_2$ quarts Chicken Broth (page 16)

$^1/_2$ pound yellow or white potatoes, peeled and diced (about $1^1/_4$ cups)

1 ounce dried mung bean threads (cellophane noodles)

2 tablespoons soy sauce

$^1/_2$ tablespoon red chili or hot bean paste

$^1/_2$ teaspoon sugar

4 scallions, thinly sliced

2 hard boiled eggs, chopped

$1^1/_2$ celery stalks, diced

1 recipe Fried Shallots (page 203)

1 lemon, cut into wedges

Remove the giblets from the chicken; discard the liver or save for another use. Wash the chicken and rub it with $^1/_2$ teaspoon salt. Set aside.

Heat the oil in a skillet over high heat. Add the chopped shallots, lemongrass, garlic, ginger, black pepper, and turmeric. Cook, stirring constantly, until the aroma is apparent, about 30 seconds. Remove from the heat.

Combine the broth and remaining $1^1/_2$ teaspoons salt with the chicken, giblets, and shallot mixture in a soup pot. Bring to a simmer and cook until the chicken is cooked through and tender, about 45 minutes. Skim often to remove any foam.

Remove the chicken from the broth and, when cool enough to handle, remove the chicken meat from the bones. Return the bones to the broth and continue to simmer 1 hour, skimming as needed. Meanwhile, dice the chicken meat and set aside.

Place the potatoes in a saucepan, cover with cold water, and bring to a simmer. Cook until tender, about 20 minutes. Drain and spread the potatoes in a single layer to cool.

Soak the bean threads in enough hot water to cover, until tender, about 5 minutes. Rinse and separate the strands under cool running water. Chop into 2-inch lengths and set aside.

When the broth has simmered for 1 hour, strain it through a fine sieve. Mix together the soy sauce, chili paste, and sugar; stir into the strained broth.

Add the chicken meat, potatoes, bean threads, scallions, egg, and celery to the broth. Bring to a simmer and add a squeeze of lemon, to taste.

Serve in heated bowls, garnished with fried shallots. Pass the lemon wedges on the side.

borscht

Borscht is one of those soups that has dozens of variations. This version of the classic Russian beet soup uses lots of vegetables and a touch of bacon for extra flavor. You can leave the bacon out and use vegetable broth if you prefer a vegetarian soup. Grating the beets into the soup releases maximum flavor. Though this recipe calls for the borscht to be served hot, it is also delicious cold.

MAKES 8 SERVINGS

2 medium beets

2 tablespoons minced bacon

2 medium onions, diced finely (about 2½ cups)

2 celery stalks, cut into matchsticks (about 1 cup)

2 parsnips, cut into matchsticks (about ⅔ cup)

1 carrot, cut into matchsticks (about ⅓ cup)

1 leek, white and light green parts, cut into matchsticks (about 1¼ cups)

½ Savoy cabbage, shredded (about 3 cups)

2 quarts Chicken or Vegetable Broth (pages 16, 20)

Sachet: 1 teaspoon dried marjoram, 4–5 parsley stems, 2 cloves peeled garlic, and 1 bay leaf enclosed in a large teaball or tied in a cheesecloth pouch

Red-wine vinegar, to taste

Salt, to taste

Freshly ground black pepper, to taste

½ cup sour cream

¼ cup minced fresh dill

Simmer the beets in enough boiling water to cover until partially cooked, 10–15 minutes. When cool enough to handle, peel and reserve (use gloves to keep your hands from turning purple).

Cook the bacon in a soup pot over medium heat until crisp, 6–8 minutes.

Add the onions, celery, parsnips, carrot, leek, and cabbage. Cover and cook over low heat, stirring occasionally, until the vegetables are translucent, about 15 minutes.

Add the broth and sachet. Bring to a simmer and cook, 10 minutes.

Grate the parboiled beets (wear gloves) directly into the soup and simmer until all the vegetables are tender, about 10 minutes.

Remove the sachet and discard. Season with the vinegar, salt, and pepper. Serve in heated bowls, garnished with sour cream and dill.

PHEASANT BORSCHT

Remove the neck and giblets from the cavity of a 2½-pound pheasant. Rinse the cavity with cold water. Place the pheasant in a soup pot and add 2 quarts chicken broth, plus more as needed, to cover the pheasant. Bring to a simmer over low heat and cook until the pheasant meat is tender, about 45 minutes, skimming as needed. Remove the pheasant from the broth and cool. Strain the broth using a fine sieve or cheesecloth-lined colander. When the pheasant is cool enough to handle, skin it and remove the meat from the carcass. Discard the skin and shred the meat. Substitute 2 quarts of the pheasant broth for the chicken or vegetable broth in the preceding recipe. Add the shredded pheasant meat to the soup just before seasoning.

vietnamese water spinach and beef soup

Water spinach is both cultivated and grows wild throughout Asia. It bears no relationship to ordinary spinach, though it is used in much the same way as spinach for some purposes. Water spinach leaves are tender and have a sweet, mild flavor and slightly slippery texture when cooked. The edible stems provide a crisp contrast to the leaves. Look for water spinach at Asian groceries. It wilts quickly, so buy only the freshest looking bunch and plan to store it no longer than two days wrapped in a plastic bag in the bottom of your refrigerator. If you cannot find water spinach, ordinary spinach makes a fine substitute.

MAKES 6 TO 8 SERVINGS

2 ounces fresh water spinach, tough stem parts trimmed, or 1 cup packed spinach leaves

1 ounce dried mung bean threads (cellophane noodles)

1 tablespoon vegetable oil

1 tablespoon sliced shallot

1/2 teaspoon minced garlic

Pinch crushed red pepper

3 ounces beef flank steak, cut into thin strips (about 1/3 cup)

1 quart Chicken Broth (page 16)

1 tablespoon soy sauce

1 tablespoon Vietnamese fish sauce *(nuoc mam)*

1 tablespoon lemon juice

1/2 teaspoon sugar

Salt, to taste

Freshly ground black pepper, to taste

2 tablespoons chopped cilantro

Bring a medium pot of water to a boil. Add the water spinach or spinach leaves and cook, just until wilted, 1–2 minutes. Remove with a slotted spoon and drain well. When cool enough to handle, squeeze the excess moisture from the spinach. Chop and set aside.

Soak the bean threads in enough hot water to cover, until tender, about 5 minutes. Rinse and separate the strands under cool running water. Chop into 2-inch pieces and set aside.

Heat the oil in large wok or soup pot over medium-high heat. Add the shallots, garlic, and red pepper. Stir-fry, 30 seconds. Add the beef and stir-fry, 1 minute. Add the broth, soy sauce, fish sauce, lemon juice, and sugar. Bring the soup to a simmer. Add spinach and season with salt and black pepper.

Distribute the bean threads evenly among heated bowls. Ladle the soup over the bean threads and garnish with the cilantro.

salmon miso soup

Miso, *which is fermented soybean paste, is a principle ingredient in Japanese cooking. It comes in a variety of flavors and colors. Most miso is quite salty, though low-salt varieties are available. Containing large amounts of protein and B vitamins, it's also highly nutritious. The variety called for in this soup, yellow* (shinshu) *miso, is very mellow as misos go. Daikon is a large, white Asian radish with a sweet flavor and crisp texture. Look for daikon and miso, as well as many of the other ingredients called for here, in Asian groceries and health-food stores. See page 42 for information on* dashi.

MAKES 8 SERVINGS

3 teaspoons vegetable oil, divided

1 egg, lightly beaten

3 tablespoons thinly sliced scallion greens, divided

$\frac{1}{2}$ teaspoon minced fresh ginger

$\frac{1}{4}$ cup diced carrot

$\frac{1}{4}$ cup diced daikon

1$\frac{1}{2}$ quarts Chicken Broth (page 16)

5 tablespoons yellow miso (shinsu)

2$\frac{1}{4}$ teaspoons instant dashi

$\frac{1}{4}$ cup dried wakame seaweed, broken into 1-inch pieces, optional

1 cup diced soft tofu

$\frac{1}{2}$ cup finely diced, fresh, boneless, skinless salmon fillet (about 3 ounces)

2$\frac{1}{4}$ teaspoons dark Asian sesame oil

$\frac{1}{4}$ teaspoon freshly ground black pepper

Heat 1 teaspoon of the oil in a nonstick omelet pan or small skillet over medium-low heat. Add the egg and cook until set on the bottom, about 1 minute. Flip the omelet and cook until completely set, 1–2 minutes. Transfer the omelet to a cutting board, dice, and set aside.

Heat the remaining 2 teaspoons oil in a large wok or soup pot. Add 1$\frac{1}{2}$ tablespoons of the scallion, and the ginger. Stir-fry briefly, about 30 seconds. Add the carrots and daikon. Stir-fry until tender, about 3 minutes.

Add the broth, miso, and dashi. Stir to combine and dissolve. Add the seaweed, if using.

Bring the soup to a simmer. Add the tofu, salmon, sesame oil, and black pepper. Simmer until the salmon is just cooked, about 1 minute.

Serve in heated bowls, garnished with the remaining scallions and the diced omelet.

crabmeat tofu soup

A primary ingredient in Japanese cooking, dashi *is a broth made by simmering flakes of dried bonito tuna* (katsuobushi) *with pieces of giant kelp* (kombu). *Instant dashi* (dashi-no-moto) *is available in liquid concentrate or powdered granules, the form used in this recipe. In the U.S., it is sometimes marketed as "bonito-flavored soup stock."* Tamari *is a Japanese soy sauce. The ingredients for this soup can be purchased at Asian groceries and some health-food stores.*

MAKES 6 SERVINGS

1¹/₂ cups packed spinach leaves, rinsed well

1 quart Chicken Broth (page 16)

1 tablespoon tamari

1¹/₂ teaspoons instant dashi granules

6 ounces soft tofu, diced

¹/₂ cup crabmeat, picked over for shells, roughly cut if pieces are large

¹/₄ cup dried wakame seaweed, broken into 1-inch pieces, optional

Salt, to taste

Freshly ground white pepper, to taste

1 egg, beaten

1¹/₂ teaspoons dark Asian sesame oil

Bring a medium pot of water to a boil. Add the spinach and cook just until wilted, 1–2 minutes. Remove the spinach with a slotted spoon and drain well. When cool enough to handle, squeeze excess moisture from the spinach. Chop and set aside.

Bring the broth to a simmer in a large wok or soup pot. Add the tamari and dashi. Stir until the dashi is dissolved. Add the tofu, crabmeat, and seaweed, if using. Season with salt and pepper.

Return the soup to a simmer. While stirring gently, pour the egg into the soup and continue to stir gently until bits of egg float to the top.

Just before serving, add the sesame oil and chopped spinach. Serve in heated bowls.

chinese hot-and-sour soup

Compared to the Thai hot-and-sour soup on page 45, which derives its heat from chile peppers and its sour from citrus, this Chinese soup is quite different, its heat due to the white and black peppercorns, and sour from two kinds of vinegar. The garnishes in the two soups are also quite different. With little flavor of their own, dried cloud ears (also known as black fungus, wood ears, or tree ears) soak up the other flavors of the soup and provide a soft, slightly rubbery textural element. Dried tiger-lily buds, also known as golden needles, add texture, too, as well as a slightly sweet or musky flavor. Find these and other ingredients not available at your supermarket in an Asian grocery.

MAKES 10 TO 12 SERVINGS

2 tablespoons dried cloud ears

2 tablespoons dried tiger-lily buds

1 tablespoon vegetable oil

1 tablespoon chopped scallion, green part only

³/₄ teaspoon minced ginger

¹/₄ pound pork butt, ground or cut into matchsticks

1¹/₂ cups shredded napa cabbage

¹/₄ cup canned bamboo shoots, drained and thinly sliced, optional

5 cups Chicken Broth (page 16)

1 cup diced soft tofu

1 tablespoon Chinese black soy sauce

1 tablespoon white vinegar

1 tablespoon rice vinegar

1 teaspoon salt, or to taste

³/₄ teaspoon freshly ground white pepper

³/₄ teaspoon freshly ground black pepper

¹/₄ cup cornstarch, dissolved in 2 tablespoons cold water

1 egg, lightly beaten

1¹/₂ teaspoons dark Asian sesame oil

¹/₃ cup chopped cilantro

Soak the cloud ears and lily buds in enough warm water to cover until softened, about 10 minutes. Drain and rinse well. Cut the stems from the cloud ears and lily buds. Cut the cloud ears into small pieces and the lily buds in half. Set aside.

Heat the oil in a large wok or soup pot over medium-high heat. Add the scallions and ginger. Stir-fry briefly, about 30 seconds. Add the pork and stir-fry until cooked through, 1–2 minutes.

Add the cloud ears, lily buds, cabbage, and bamboo shoots, if using. Stir-fry until the cabbage is tender, about 2 minutes.

Add the broth and tofu and bring to a simmer. Add the soy sauce, white vinegar, rice vinegar, salt, white pepper, and black pepper.

Stir the cornstarch-water mixture to recombine. While stirring the soup, add about ¹/₂ of the cornstarch mixture. Continue to stir until the soup returns to a simmer and thickens. The soup should have a slightly thick consistency. If needed, add the remaining cornstarch mixture in small amounts to the soup, while stirring. Let the soup return to a simmer each time. (Depending on how thick you like your soup, you may not need to use all the cornstarch.)

Stir the egg and sesame oil into soup. Return to a simmer. Serve in heated bowls, garnished with the cilantro.

thai hot-and-sour soup

Thai hot-and-sour soup creates a fascinating interplay of spicy-hot chile and sour-citrus flavor. All the ingredients are crucial to the overall flavor, so don't leave anything out. You can find them at Asian groceries and some specialty markets. Once you have all your ingredients assembled, this soup is a snap to put together.

MAKES 8 SERVINGS

¼ pound small (30–35 count per pound) shrimp, peeled and butterflied

2 ounces thin rice noodles (rice vermicelli)

2 quarts Chicken Broth (page 16)

1 stalk fresh lemongrass, cut into 2-inch pieces, smashed

¼ cup Thai fish sauce *(nam pla)*

2 tablespoons chili oil

2 teaspoons lime zest

½ pickled chili

Juice of 1 lemon

Juice of 1 lime

⅓ cup drained, canned straw mushrooms

¼ cup chopped cilantro

Bring a medium pot of water to a boil. Add the shrimp and boil until cooked through, about 3 minutes. Use a slotted spoon to transfer the shrimp to a colander. Rinse under cold water, drain, and set aside. Cook the rice noodles in the same pot of boiling water until tender, 2–3 minutes. Drain, rinse under cold water, and drain again. Set aside.

Combine the broth with the lemongrass, fish sauce, chili oil, lime zest, pickled chili, lemon juice, and lime juice in a wok or soup pot. Bring to a simmer and cook, 10 minutes. Strain or use a slotted spoon to remove the lemongrass.

Distribute the rice noodles, shrimp, mushrooms, and cilantro among 8 heated soup bowls. Ladle the broth into the bowls and serve.

egg drop soup

This homemade version of the Chinese restaurant favorite is quick and easy to make. Adding the cornstarch gradually allows you to thicken the soup to suit your taste.

MAKES 8 SERVINGS

3 teaspoons vegetable oil

5 tablespoons thinly sliced scallion, green part only

1 1/2 teaspoons minced fresh ginger root

2 quarts Chicken Broth (page 16)

1 teaspoon salt, or to taste

1/4 teaspoon freshly ground white pepper, or to taste

1/4 cup cornstarch, dissolved in 2 tablespoons cold water

2 eggs, beaten

Heat the oil in a large wok or soup pot over medium-high heat. Add 1 tablespoon of the scallion, and the ginger. Stir-fry until softened, about 1 minute.

Add the broth and bring to a boil. Season with the salt and pepper.

Stir the cornstarch mixture to recombine any starch that has settled to the bottom. While stirring the soup, add about 1/2 of the cornstarch mixture to the soup. Continue to stir until the soup comes back to a simmer and thickens. The soup should have a slightly thick consistency. If needed, add the remaining cornstarch mixture in small amounts to the soup while stirring. Let the soup return to a simmer each time before adding more cornstarch. (Depending on how thick you like your soup, you may not need to use all the cornstarch.)

Beat the eggs gently in a bowl. Pour them into the soup, while slowly stirring with a spoon, breaking the eggs into pieces.

Serve in heated bowls, garnished with the remaining scallion.

wonton soup

Though it's easy enough to order wonton soup from your neighborhood Chinese takeout, you may find that this freshly made wonton soup beats the restaurant version. Making the wontons is fun; it takes a bit of time, but your speed will increase as you get the hang of it. You can tightly wrap and freeze any leftover wonton wrappers for next time. Once the wontons are made, the soup comes together in a snap. Look for any hard-to-find ingredients at an Asian grocery.

MAKES 8 SERVINGS

FOR THE WONTONS:

3 ounces ground pork (about $^1/_3$ cup)

$^1/_2$ cup finely chopped napa cabbage

2 tablespoons Chicken Broth (page 16)

1 tablespoon minced scallion, green part only

$^1/_2$ teaspoon minced fresh ginger

$^3/_4$ teaspoon soy sauce

$^3/_4$ teaspoon dark Asian sesame oil

Pinch salt

Pinch freshly ground white pepper

32 wonton wrappers (3-inch diameter)

1 egg, beaten

FOR THE SOUP:

2 teaspoons vegetable oil, divided

1 teaspoon minced scallion, green part only

$^1/_2$ teaspoon minced fresh ginger root

5 cups Chicken Broth (page 16)

1$^1/_2$ teaspoons Chinese black soy sauce

Salt and freshly ground white pepper, to taste

1 egg, lightly beaten

1 ounce ham, cut into thin strips (about $^1/_4$ cup)

$^1/_4$ cup watercress sprigs, optional

MAKE THE WONTONS:

Combine the pork, cabbage, broth, scallion, ginger, soy sauce, sesame oil, salt, and pepper. Mix well. Place $^1/_2$ teaspoon of the mixture in the center of a wonton wrapper. Brush the edges of the wrapper with beaten egg and fold it into a triangle. Twist and press the two triangle points together to form a wonton. Repeat with the remaining filling and wrappers to make about 32 wontons.

Bring a large pot of water to a boil. Cook the wontons in boiling water until they float, about 2 minutes. Drain and rinse under cool water. Transfer to a bowl, cover, and set aside.

MAKE THE SOUP:

Heat 1 teaspoon of the oil in a large wok or soup pot over medium-high heat. Add the scallion and ginger and stir-fry, 30 seconds. Add the broth and bring to a simmer. Add the soy sauce and salt and pepper. Keep hot.

Heat the remaining oil in a nonstick omelet pan or small skillet over medium-low heat. Add the beaten egg and cook until set on the bottom, about 1 minute. Flip the omelet and cook until completely set, 1–2 minutes. Transfer to a cutting board and slice into thin strips.

Distribute the wontons evenly among heated bowls (at least 4 per bowl). Ladle the soup over the wontons and garnish with the omelet strips, ham, and watercress, if using.

mussel soup

The hairy, inedible filaments that protrude from a mussel are known, collectively, as a beard. *To debeard a mussel, pinch the filaments between your thumb and forefinger and pull firmly. Debearding a mussel kills it, so wait until just before cooking to perform this step. You can substitute a variety of seafood for the mussels, if you like. Any white fish, such as flounder, halibut, or monkfish, works well, as does shelled and deveined shrimp. Freshly shucked clams or oysters are tasty in this soup, too.*

MAKES 8 SERVINGS

1/2 cup white wine

1 shallot, minced

1 bay leaf

1 fresh thyme sprig, optional

50 mussels (about 3 pounds), debearded and scrubbed well under cold running water

1/4 cup olive oil

1 small onion, finely diced (about 1 cup)

1 leek, white and light green parts, finely diced (about 1 1/4 cups)

1 celery stalk, finely diced (about 1/2 cup)

2 garlic cloves, minced

2 cups canned plum tomatoes, drained, seeded, and chopped, juices reserved

1–2 cups Fish Broth (page 19) or water, as needed

1 teaspoon dried basil

Salt, to taste

Freshly ground black pepper, to taste

1/2 teaspoon grated lemon zest

1/4 cup chopped fresh basil or parsley

8 Breadsticks (page 186)

In a pot large enough to accommodate the mussels, combine the wine, shallot, bay leaf, thyme sprig, if using, and enough water to raise the liquid level to about 1 inch. Bring to a boil. Add the mussels, cover, and steam until they open, about 5 minutes. Use a slotted spoon to transfer the mussels to a bowl, and let cool slightly. Remove the mussels from their shells and set aside (discard the shells). Strain the cooking liquid through a coffee filter and set aside.

Heat the olive oil in a soup pot over medium heat. Add the onion, leek, celery, and garlic. Cover the pot, reduce the heat to medium-low, and cook until the vegetables are translucent, 6–8 minutes.

Combine the mussel cooking liquid with the reserved tomato juice. Add enough fish broth or water to make 1 quart. Add this mixture along with the tomatoes and basil to the soup pot. Bring to a simmer and cook, partially covered, 10–12 minutes.

Add the mussels and cover the pot. Simmer until the mussels are heated through, about 2 minutes.

Season with the salt, pepper, and lemon zest. Serve in heated bowls, garnished with fresh basil or parsley, and accompanied by breadsticks.

VARIATIONS

Try one or more of the following: Add 1/2 teaspoon of saffron with the tomatoes; substitute 1/4 cup Pernod and 1/4 cup dry vermouth for the white wine; add a sachet containing 1/2 teaspoon each of anise and fennel seeds, and 1 clove of peeled garlic, at the same time that the tomatoes are added.

CHAPTER THREE

hearty soups

MINESTRONE ❖ POTAGE AU PISTOU ❖ HAM BONE & COLLARD GREENS SOUP ❖ MINNESOTA

WILD RICE SOUP ❖ CALDO VERDE ❖ GOULASH SOUP ❖ CIOPPINO ❖ SHIITAKE MUSHROOM

& YUKON GOLD POTATO SOUP WITH BACON ❖ TORTILLA SOUP ❖ POSOLE-POBLANO SOUP

WITH SMOKED PORK & JALAPEÑO JACK CHEESE ❖ MUSHROOM BARLEY SOUP ❖ CORNED BEEF,

BARLEY, AND CABBAGE SOUP ❖ CURRIED EGGPLANT-AND-LENTIL SOUP ❖ MULLIGATAWNY

SOUP ❖ LEBLEBI ❖ HLELEM ❖ FRENCH LENTIL SOUP ❖ RED LENTIL SOUP ❖ SHRIMP AND

ANDOUILLE GUMBO ❖ SEAFOOD GUMBO ❖ CALLALOO

THE SOUPS FEATURED IN THIS CHAPTER are more robust than the broth-style soups in chapter two. These are nourishing soups that are a meal by themselves, especially when paired with some bread or crackers. Though most are based on a flavorful broth like the soups in chapter two, these substantial soups tend to be abundant with vegetables, meats or seafood, and pasta, grains, or legumes.

MAIN INGREDIENTS FOR HEARTY SOUPS

A variety of broths and other liquids, including water, vegetable essences, or juices, are used as the base for hearty soups. As always, be sure to test the quality of any broth that has been refrigerated before making your soup. If you are preparing large quantities of soup, it can be helpful to bring the broth to a simmer over low heat while preparing the other ingredients. This will help reduce overall cooking time, because the soup will come to the correct cooking temperature more quickly.

Though frozen vegetables are sometimes appropriate, fresh vegetables are almost always preferred. Trim and cut the vegetables as instructed by the recipe. Because the vegetables that are cooked in the soup are part of the finished dish, it is important to make the cuts neat and uniform. In this way, you can be certain the items will cook uniformly and that they will have an attractive appearance.

Most hearty soups also include meat, poultry, or fish. Some call for a combination— for example, gumbo typically includes a combination of seafood, chicken, and/or pork sausage. Be sure these ingredients are fresh and trimmed well of skin, bones, and any excess fat. Scrub shellfish to remove grit.

Beans, whole grains, pastas, rice, or other similar ingredients are frequently included in hearty soups. The starch they contain tends to make these soups slightly thick. These ingredients can either be cooked directly in the soup, or cooked separately and added near the end of cooking time. If these ingredients are cooked in the soup, however, be sure to allow for the amount of liquid they will absorb, and be aware that the soup will be less clear.

SUPPORTING FLAVORS

Aromatic combinations of herbs, spices, and other ingredients are added at specific points during the cooking time so that they will surrender the best flavor. Prepare a sachet or add these ingredients directly to the soup as directed. In addition to the ingredients called for in a recipe, you may opt to include other herbs, herb stems, spices, dried or fresh mushrooms, and/or chiles to achieve a particular flavor in the finished soup. Fortified wines, vinegar, or citrus juices are all common choices for last-minute flavor adjustment.

Croutons are a common garnish for hearty soups. Other garnishes, such as pesto, grated cheese, or even beaten eggs, can be added just before serving. Purees of red peppers, chiles, tomato, or sorrel may also be added at the last moment for a dash of color and flavor.

EVALUATING THE QUALITY OF HEARTY SOUPS

Hearty soups should be full of flavor, which reflects the main ingredients used and should be well balanced. All the ingredients should be tender but never mushy. Properly cooked vegetables (especially green ones) should be brightly colored, with no graying.

Despite your best efforts, occasionally a hearty soup may not turn out quite as expected. Following are the most common problems that occur with hearty soups, and some of their causes.

- *Harsh flavor.* If the flavor is too harsh, the wrong ratio of ingredients was used, the vegetables were not properly sweated, or the soup was not cooked long enough.

- *Inappropriate color.* If the soup appears muddy or gray, the vegetables have probably been overcooked. If pastas or grains have been cooked directly in the soup, they may have been overcooked to the point that they have begun to break down. Ideally, these ingredients should be added to the soup in such a manner that they will cook fully but will not overcook.

basic hearty soup method

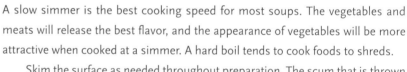

➥ *Cook the aromatic vegetables in fat.*

Heat some oil and/or sauté some bacon (fig. 1), then add onions, garlic, leeks, carrots, celery, and parsnips. These are often included in the basic ingredients of hearty soups. Cooking them gently in a small amount of oil, butter, or rendered bacon or salt pork begins the process of releasing their flavors into the soup (fig. 2). Note that some tender vegetables, such as broccoli florets, asparagus tips, and other delicate types, are not generally cooked at this point. They are added later, at staggered intervals, according to individual cooking times. For some hearty soups, you may wish to add tomatoes and cook until lightly browned (fig. 3).

➥ *Add the liquid and bring to a simmer.*

A slow simmer is the best cooking speed for most soups. The vegetables and meats will release the best flavor, and the appearance of vegetables will be more attractive when cooked at a simmer. A hard boil tends to cook foods to shreds.

Skim the surface as needed throughout preparation. The scum that is thrown by the soup needs to be removed for the best finished quality.

4.

5.

6.

 Add the remaining ingredients at appropriate intervals.

Depending upon the style of soup you are preparing, additional ingredients, such as chicken pieces, corned beef brisket, dense vegetables, grains, or legumes may be added at the same time as the liquid (fig. 4). Keep the overall cooking time of the soup in mind, as well as that required by individual ingredients. Refer to recipes for more guidance.

Delicate vegetables, such as green peas, corn, or asparagus tips are usually added near the end of cooking time. Meats, vegetables, pastas, grains, or legumes that have been cooked separately are also usually added in the last few minutes of cooking time (fig. 5). Sachets are generally added so that they will cook just long enough to release flavor into the soup. Overcooking these ingredients can deaden their flavor.

 Simmer until the flavor is fully developed and all the ingredients are tender.

It is important to taste the soup frequently as it cook, which will allow you to make adjustments if necessary during cooking time. It will also tell you when the soup has reached its peak flavor.

Once the soup has reached that point, it is ready for final seasoning and garnishing (fig. 6). Or, it may be properly cooled and stored following the procedures outlined in chapter 1.

minestrone

Minestrone, *literally, "big soup,"* is an Italian classic packed with vegetables, pasta, and beans. A bowl of minestrone can be a meal all by itself. There is no one right way to make minestrone. Recipes vary from cook to cook according to individual preferences, so feel free to improvise with other vegetables, beans, or pasta shapes to suit your taste. Pancetta *is a type of Italian bacon. It can usually be found in delis and butcher shops, but, if it is unavailable in your area, you can omit it or substitute regular bacon.*

MAKES 8 SERVINGS

2 tablespoons olive oil

1 ounce pancetta, chopped (5–6 thin slices)

1¹/₂ cups chopped green cabbage

1 cup chopped onions

1 cup sliced carrots

¹/₄ cup chopped celery

2 garlic cloves, minced

1 cup chopped, drained, canned plum tomatoes

2 quarts Chicken Broth (page 16)

¹/₂ cup peeled, diced potato

1 ounce Parmesan cheese rind

3 ounces vermicelli or angel hair pasta, broken into 2-inch pieces (about ³/₄ cup)

¹/₄ cup drained, canned chickpeas

¹/₃ cup drained, canned kidney beans

¹/₃ cup Pesto (page 200)

¹/₂ teaspoon salt, or to taste

¹/₄ teaspoon freshly ground black pepper, or to taste

Freshly grated Parmesan cheese, as needed

Heat the oil in a soup pot over medium heat. Add the pancetta and cook until the fat melts, 3–5 minutes. Do not brown.

Add the cabbage, onions, carrots, celery, and garlic. Cook until the onions are translucent, 6–8 minutes. Add the tomatoes and sauté another 2–3 minutes.

Add the broth, potato, and Parmesan cheese rind. Bring to a simmer and cook until the vegetables are tender, about 30 minutes. Do not overcook.

Meanwhile, cook the vermicelli according to package directions, until tender. Drain.

When the vegetables in the soup are tender, add the cooked vermicelli, chickpeas, and kidney beans. Remove and discard the Parmesan rind.

Season the soup to taste with the pesto, salt, and pepper. Serve in heated bowls, sprinkled with cheese.

FACING PAGE: Chopping the pancetta (top left); cutting the rind from the Parmesan cheese to flavor the minestrone (top right); breaking long strands of vermicelli into bite-sized pieces (bottom left); chopping the cabbage (bottom right)

potage au pistou
(vegetable soup with garlic and basil)

Pistou is both the name of this soup and the garlic and basil condiment used to season it. Pistou, the condiment, is the French version of Italy's pesto. Pistou, the soup, is the French version of Italy's minestrone. You can substitute 1½ cups canned navy beans, drained and rinsed, for dried. Simply add them to the soup, along with the vermicelli. This soup is best in late summer, when many of the ingredients can be purchased from your local farmstand or picked from your garden. Served with a loaf of crusty bread (with olive oil for dipping) and a bottle of chilled dry white wine, it makes a fine meal.

MAKES 8 TO 10 SERVINGS

³/₄ cup dried navy beans, soaked overnight in 3 cups of water

2 tablespoons olive oil

3 carrots, diced (about 1 cup)

2 leeks, white and light green parts, diced (about 2½ cups)

1 onion, diced (about 1¼ cups)

2½ quarts Chicken Broth (page 16), heated

Pinch saffron threads, optional

6 ounces green beans, cut into 1-inch lengths (about 1 cup)

1 yellow or white potato, peeled and diced (about 1 cup)

1 medium zucchini, diced (about 1 cup)

2 ounces vermicelli or angel-hair pasta, broken into 2-inch lengths (about ³/₄ cup)

2 ripe tomatoes, peeled, seeded, and diced (page 36, about 2 cups)

Salt, to taste

Freshly ground black pepper, to taste

1 recipe Pistou (page 200), or to taste

Drain the beans and place in a large saucepan. Add 1 quart water, and bring to a simmer. Cook until tender, about 1 hour, adding more water, if necessary, to keep the beans covered.

Heat the oil in a soup pot over medium heat. Add the carrots, leeks, and onion. Cook until the onion is translucent, about 10 minutes. Add the broth and the saffron, if using, to the vegetables, bring to a simmer, and cook, 10 minutes.

Add the green beans, potato, and zucchini. Continue to simmer, 10 minutes.

Add the vermicelli and simmer until tender, about 8 minutes.

Drain the beans of their cooking liquid and add them to the soup along with the tomatoes. Season to taste with salt and pepper and continue to simmer, 1 minute.

Add the pistou, to taste, just before serving. Serve in heated bowls.

ham bone and collard greens soup

This hearty southern-style soup is packed with vitamin- and mineral-rich collard greens. Ham-bone soup was originally meant as a means to get the most meal mileage from a ham, but we have developed this recipe using a smoked ham hock (which should be available from your supermarket), so you don't have to purchase and eat a whole ham to make the soup. If you do happen to have a meaty ham bone, though, by all means use it instead of the ham hock. Ham hocks can be quite salty, so use salt-free homemade broth or a reduced-sodium canned variety to make this soup.

MAKES 8 SERVINGS

1 smoked ham hock

3 quarts Chicken Broth (page 16)

1¼ pounds collard greens

1 tablespoon vegetable oil

¼ cup minced salt pork (about 3 ounces)

1 onion, minced (about 1¼ cups)

1 celery stalk, minced (about ½ cup)

½ cup all-purpose flour

Sachet: 5–6 black peppercorns, 4 parsley stems, and 1 fresh sprig or ½ teaspoon dried thyme enclosed in a large teaball or tied in a cheesecloth pouch

½ cup heavy cream

4 teaspoons malt vinegar, or to taste

Tabasco sauce, to taste

Place the ham hock and broth in a pot large enough to accommodate both. Bring to a simmer and cook, partially covered, 1½ hours. Remove the ham hock from the broth and allow both to cool slightly.

Meanwhile, bring a large pot of salted water to a boil. Cut the tough ribs and stems from the collard greens. Plunge the greens into boiling water and cook, 10 minutes. Drain and cool slightly. Chop the greens coarsely and set aside.

Heat the oil in a soup pot over medium heat. Add the salt pork and cook until crisp, 3–5 minutes. Add the onions and celery and cook, stirring occasionally, until tender, about 5 minutes.

Add the flour and cook, stirring frequently, 5 minutes. Gradually add the broth, whisking constantly to work out any lumps of flour. Bring to a simmer and add the collard greens, ham hock, and sachet. Cook 1 hour.

Remove and discard the sachet. Remove the ham hock and cool slightly. Trim away the skin and fat and dice the lean meat. Return the meat to the soup.

Add the cream and season with vinegar and Tabasco. Serve in heated bowls.

minnesota wild rice soup

This rich soup, which is packed with vegetables, is an unusual way to enjoy wild rice. Wild rice contains a substance that produces a unique texture in this soup, not unlike a chowder. Incidentally, wild rice is not rice; it's actually a long-grain marsh grass native to the Great Lakes region of the United States. Many local Native Americans earn their living harvesting wild rice, which is why it's sometimes known as Indian rice. Clean wild rice before cooking by placing it in a bowl with plenty of cold water. Give the rice a stir, then set the bowl aside for a few minutes to let any debris float to the surface. Pour off the water and proceed with the recipe.

MAKES 8 SERVINGS

2 tablespoons unsalted butter

3 carrots, finely diced (about 1 cup)

2 leeks, white and light green parts, finely diced (about 2 ½ cups)

2 celery stalks, finely diced (about 1 cup)

¼ cup all-purpose flour

2 quarts Chicken Broth (page 16)

¾ cup wild rice

½ teaspoon salt, or to taste

¾ cup heavy cream, hot

3 tablespoons dry sherry

¼ cup minced chives

3 tablespoons chopped parsley

Heat the butter in a soup pot over medium heat. Add the carrots, leeks, and celery. Cook until softened, about 5 minutes.

Reduce the heat to low, add the flour, and stir well. Cook gently, about 3 minutes, stirring constantly.

Add the broth gradually, whisking well with each addition to eliminate flour lumps. Bring to a simmer.

Add the wild rice and salt. Continue to simmer until the rice is tender, but still somewhat chewy, about 45 minutes.

Stir in the heated cream and sherry. Season with salt. Serve in heated bowls, garnished with chives and parsley.

caldo verde (portuguese potato kale soup)

Caldo verde, *literally, "green soup," is a robust, incredibly satisfying concoction of kale, garlic, and smoky meats in a silky pureed potato soup base. Served with a loaf of Portuguese bread, it makes a meal. Linguiça is a Portuguese garlic sausage that can be found in many supermarkets and Latin-American markets.*

MAKES 8 SERVINGS

1 tablespoon olive oil

¹/₂ leek, white and light green part, diced (about ³/₄ cup)

¹/₂ onion, diced (about ³/₄ cup)

¹/₂ celery stalk, diced (about ¹/₄ cup)

5 cups Chicken Broth (page 16)

4 russet potatoes, peeled, cut in sixths

1 smoked ham hock

¹/₄ pound fresh kale (about 1¹/₂ cups)

2 ounces linguiça sausage, diced (about ¹/₂ link)

¹/₂ bay leaf

Salt, to taste

Freshly ground black pepper, to taste

Heat the oil in a soup pot over medium heat. Add the leek, onion, and celery. Cook, stirring occasionally, until the onion is translucent, 4–6 minutes.

Add the broth, potatoes, and ham hock. Bring to a simmer and cook until all are very tender, about 40 minutes.

Meanwhile, bring a large pot of salted water to a rolling boil. Use a paring knife to cut the tough stems from the kale leaves. Blanch the kale in boiling water until it wilts, about 3 minutes. Drain the kale, run it under cold water to stop the cooking, and drain again. Slice the kale into thin shreds.

Remove the ham hock from the soup base. Puree the soup base and return to a simmer.

When cool enough to handle, remove the meat from the ham hock and dice. Add the ham hock meat, sliced kale, sausage, and bay leaf to the soup base. Season with salt and pepper, and simmer, 15–20 minutes. Serve in heated bowls.

goulash soup

Reminiscent of the paprika-flavored Hungarian stew of the same name (gulyás in Hungarian), this thick soup is robust enough to be a meal by itself. Serve it with a dab of sour cream, if you wish, and accompany it with lots of dark pumpernickel bread and dark beer.

MAKES 8 SERVINGS

6 tablespoons minced salt pork, slab bacon, or fat back

1 pound beef or veal chuck, cut into ¹/₂-inch cubes

2 onions, finely diced (about 2¹/₂ cups)

2 tablespoons red-wine vinegar

2 tablespoons all-purpose flour

1 tablespoon hot paprika

³/₄ cup tomato puree

1 quart Beef Broth (page 18)

Sachet: 1 teaspoon each caraway seeds, dried marjoram, and thyme, 4 fresh parsley stems, 2 cloves peeled garlic, and 1 bay leaf enclosed in a large teaball or tied in a cheesecloth pouch

2 yellow or white potatoes, peeled and cut into ¹/₂-inch cubes

Salt, to taste

Freshly ground black pepper, to taste

¹/₄ cup finely sliced scallion, green part only, or chives

Sauté the salt pork in a soup pot over medium heat, until the bits of pork are crisp and the fat has rendered, 4–5 minutes.

Add the cubed beef or veal and sauté in the fat until the meat begins to brown, 3–4 minutes. Add the onions and cook, covered, over medium-low heat until the onions are translucent, 8–10 minutes.

Add the vinegar and boil over high heat until the liquid begins to reduce, about 2 minutes. Add the flour and stir with a wooden spoon over medium heat, 1 more minute. Stir in the paprika, then the tomato puree, and mix thoroughly. Cook 2–3 minutes.

Add the broth and sachet. Bring the soup to a simmer and cook until the meat is almost tender, about 30 minutes. Add the potatoes and simmer until tender, about 20 minutes. Remove and discard any fat on the surface of the soup using a shallow spoon.

Season with salt and pepper. Serve in heated bowls, garnished with sliced scallions or chives.

VARIATIONS

Replace the beef broth with 1 quart dark beer. Add 1 finely diced red bell pepper at the same time as the onion. Substitute sweet paprika for hot paprika, and garnish with chopped dill or scallion.

cioppino

A savory tomato broth full of seafood and vegetables, cioppino is an American original created in San Francisco by Italian immigrants. It's a meal in and of itself. Although not traditional, you can substitute 1 cup lump crabmeat for the whole crabs. If you purchase fennel with the tops still attached, save some of the nicest-looking sprigs for garnishing. Serve the cioppino with large garlic toasts or crusty sourdough bread.

MAKES 8 TO 10 SERVINGS

2 tablespoons olive oil

2 bunches scallions, sliced (1½ cups)

2 green peppers, diced (about 2 cups)

1 onion, diced (about 1¼ cups)

1¼ cups diced fennel bulb (about 5 ounces)

5 garlic cloves, minced

1 cup white wine

1 quart Fish Broth (page 19)

8 cups canned Italian plum tomatoes, drained and chopped

½ cup tomato puree

2 bay leaves

½ teaspoon salt, or to taste

Freshly ground black pepper, to taste

20 littleneck clams, scrubbed well

3 steamed hardshell crabs, fresh cooked or frozen, thawed

20 medium shrimp, peeled and deveined

1¼ pounds swordfish or halibut steaks, diced

3 tablespoons shredded basil

Heat the oil in a soup pot over medium heat. Add the scallions, peppers, onion, and fennel. Cook, stirring occasionally, until the onion is translucent, 6–8 minutes.

Add the garlic and cook, 1 minute.

Add the white wine, bring to a boil, and cook until the volume of the wine is reduced by about half, 4–6 minutes.

Add the fish broth, tomatoes, tomato puree, and bay leaves. Cover the pot and simmer the mixture slowly, about 45 minutes. Add a small amount of water, if necessary. Cioppino should be more a broth than a stew.

Season with salt and pepper. Remove and discard the bay leaves.

Add the clams and simmer about 10 minutes. Discard any clams that do not open.

Separate the claws from the crabs and cut the bodies in half. Add the crab pieces, shrimp, and swordfish to the soup. Simmer until the fish is just cooked through, about 5 minutes.

Add the basil and adjust the seasoning, if necessary. Serve in heated bowls or soup plates.

shiitake mushroom and yukon gold potato soup with bacon

This hearty yet low-fat soup is guaranteed to satisfy hunger during the chilly fall and winter months. Pancetta is an Italian bacon that is tied in a roll as it is cured, causing it to have a spiral appearance when sliced. Unlike most American bacon, it is not smoked. Pancetta is available from specialty and butcher shops, as well as many supermarket delis. If you cannot find it, substitute 1 slice of regular bacon.

MAKES 8 SERVINGS

One $1/4$-inch-thick piece pancetta, chopped finely (about 1 ounce)

1 carrot, diced (about $1/3$ cup)

1 celery stalk, large outer veins trimmed, diced (about $1/2$ cup)

$1/2$ onion, diced (about $1/3$ cup)

$1/2$ yellow turnip, diced (about $1 1/2$ cups)

2 cups sliced fresh shiitake mushrooms (about 6 ounces)

1 pound Yukon Gold potatoes, peeled and diced

6 cups Vegetable Broth (page 20)

2 tablespoons chopped, fresh flat-leaf parsley

2 tablespoons chopped, fresh marjoram

Salt, to taste

Freshly ground black pepper, to taste

Cook the pancetta in a soup pot over low heat, until all the fat is melted and the meat begins to crisp, 6–8 minutes.

Add the carrot, celery, onion, and turnip. Cover and cook until softened, about 3 minutes.

Add the mushrooms, potatoes, and broth. Bring to a simmer and cook until the potatoes are tender, 10–12 minutes.

Add the herbs and season with salt and pepper. Serve in heated bowls.

tortilla soup

This soup, fragrant with cilantro, chili powder, and cumin, is both flavored and thickened with corn tortillas. Toasting the tortillas before grinding them helps develop their fullest flavor. Garnished with avocado, cheese, chicken, and toasted tortilla strips, this soup can be the center of a light meal, rounded out with a green salad.

MAKES 6 SERVINGS

4 corn tortillas

2 teaspoons vegetable oil

³/₄ cup finely grated or pureed onion

1 garlic clove, finely minced (about ¹/₂ teaspoon)

³/₄ cup tomato puree

1 tablespoon chopped, fresh cilantro leaves

1¹/₂ teaspoons mild chili powder

1 teaspoon ground cumin

6 cups Chicken Broth (page 16)

1 bay leaf

2 tablespoons grated cheddar cheese

¹/₂ cup shredded cooked chicken breast (from about ¹/₂ breast)

¹/₂ cup diced avocado (see note)

Preheat the oven to 300°F. Cut the tortillas into matchsticks. Place them in an even layer on a baking sheet and toast in the oven, about 15 minutes. Or, toast strips by sautéing them in a dry skillet over medium heat, tossing frequently. Reserve about ¹/₂ cup of the strips for a garnish. Crush the remainder in a food processor or blender.

Heat the oil in a soup pot over medium heat. Add the onion and garlic and cook, stirring frequently, until they have a sweet aroma, 5–6 minutes.

Add the tomato puree and continue to cook, 3 minutes. Add the cilantro, chili powder, and cumin and cook for another 2 minutes.

Add the broth, crushed tortillas, and bay leaf. Stir well, bring the soup to a simmer and cook for about 25–30 minutes. Strain the soup through a sieve.

Serve the soup in heated bowls, garnished with the shredded chicken, cheddar cheese, reserved tortilla strips, and diced avocado.

NOTE

Avocado will turn brown if it is cut very far in advance. Avoid cutting the avocado more than 1 hour before you will need it. Once you cut it, sprinkle the diced flesh with a little lemon or lime juice and toss gently to coat all the pieces. Cover and keep refrigerated. If avocados are not in season or are unavailable, substitute peeled, seeded, and diced tomatoes or cucumbers.

ALTERNATE GARNISH

Instead of making tortilla strips, cut one of the tortillas into wedges and toast them in the oven. Mash the avocado with a little lime juice and some diced tomato to make guacamole. When ready to serve, place a dollop of the guacamole on the tortilla wedges and float these "croutons" on top of the soup. Scatter grated cheese over all. Omit the shredded chicken if desired.

posole-poblano soup with smoked pork and jalapeño jack cheese

Traditionally served at Christmas, this thick Mexican soup is full of deep, complex flavors. Some of the ingredients may be unfamiliar to you, but they should not be difficult to find either at a supermarket or Latin-American grocery. Poblanos are dark-green fresh chiles that range from mild to quite spicy. Anchos are dried, ripe poblanos. Roasting (the poblanos) and toasting (the anchos) intensifies their flavors. Hominy (corn from which the hull and germ have been removed) is available canned in either gold or yellow varieties. If you have a good butcher or smokehouse nearby, you might be able to get some smoked pork shoulder. Otherwise, most supermarkets sell smoked pork chops. Masa harina (dough flour) is made from the dried dough used to make corn tortillas. It provides flavor and a slight thickening effect, but you can omit it and still have a delicious soup. Quaker makes masa harina, but purchase a Mexican brand, such as Manteca, if you can.

MAKES 6 SERVINGS

2 poblano chiles

4 teaspoons corn oil; divided

1 ancho chile

10 ounces smoked pork, diced (about 2½ cups)

Salt, to taste

Freshly ground black pepper, to taste

1 onion, diced (about 1¼ cups)

2 garlic cloves, minced

1 jalapeño pepper, seeded and minced

3 tablespoons masa harina, optional

2 tablespoons tomato paste

1½ quarts Chicken Broth (page 16), divided

1 teaspoon dried oregano

1 teaspoon dried thyme

¾ cup canned hominy, rinsed and drained

Preheat the broiler. Brush the poblanos with 1 teaspoon of the oil. Place the poblanos under the broiler and turn them as they roast so that they blacken evenly on all sides. Put the poblanos in a bowl and cover, letting them steam for 10 minutes, then remove them from the bowl and pull off the skins. Use the back of a knife to scrape away any bits that don't come away easily. Remove the seeds, ribs, and stem from poblanos. Chop flesh coarsely. Set aside.

Heat a cast-iron or other very heavy skillet over high heat. Remove the stem and seeds from the ancho and straighten it into a single layer. Toast the ancho by placing it in the hot skillet and pressing down hard with a metal spatula, until it crackles and a wisp of smoke rises, 3–5 seconds. Flip over and repeat on the other side. Chop the ancho coarsely and set aside.

Heat the remaining oil in a soup pot over medium heat. Season the pork cubes with salt and pepper and add to the pot. Cook until the pork is well browned, about 5 minutes. Add the onion and continue to cook, 5 minutes. Add the garlic and jalapeño pepper and cook, 1 minute more. Add the masa harina, if using, and cook for 1 minute. Add the tomato paste and cook for 1 minute.

Juice of 1 lime, or to taste

½ cup grated jalapeño jack cheese

2 tablespoons chopped fresh cilantro

½ cup diced jicama, optional

1 tomatillo, papery hull removed, washed, and diced, optional

2–3 radishes, diced or cut into matchsticks, optional

Add 4½ cups of the broth along with the oregano and thyme. Bring to a simmer and cook, at least 20 minutes.

Meanwhile, place the remaining broth and the ancho chile in a saucepan. Bring to a simmer and cook until the chile is quite tender, about 15 minutes. Puree the ancho and broth in a blender.

When the soup has simmered for at least 20 minutes, add the ancho puree. Continue to simmer, 15 minutes.

Add the poblanos and hominy. Simmer, 10 minutes.

Just before serving, season with lime juice, salt, and pepper. Serve in heated bowls, garnished with cheese and cilantro, as well as the jicama, tomatillo, and radish, if using. Or, put the garnishes in small bowls and pass them on the side.

mushroom barley soup

Fresh white mushrooms are used in this version of a traditional winter soup, but feel free to bolster the flavor by incorporating your favorite fresh or dried wild mushrooms. A splash of sherry added at the last moment brings this humble dish up to a whole new level. This soup will mellow and deepen in flavor if it is prepared a day ahead. It will also thicken slightly; to adjust the consistency, add a little water or broth and reheat.

MAKES 8 SERVINGS

1 tablespoon vegetable oil

1 onion, finely diced (about 1¹/₄ cups)

1 carrot, finely diced (about ¹/₃ cup)

1 celery stalk, finely diced (about ¹/₂ cup)

1 parsnip, finely diced (about ¹/₃ cup, optional

3 cups sliced white mushrooms (about 10 ounces)

2 quarts Chicken Broth (page 16)

³/₄ cup pearl barley

¹/₂ teaspoon salt, or to taste

¹/₂ teaspoon freshly ground black pepper, or to taste

1 tablespoon chopped parsley

2 tablespoons dry sherry or sherry wine vinegar, optional

Heat the oil in a soup pot over medium heat. Add the onion and cook, stirring frequently, until golden brown, about 10 minutes.

Add the carrot, celery, parsnip, if using, and mushrooms. Stir well to combine with the onion. Cover and cook over low heat, for 3–4 minutes.

Remove the cover and add the broth and barley. Bring to a simmer and cook until the barley is tender, about 30 minutes.

Season with salt and pepper. Stir in the parsley. Stir in the sherry or vinegar, if using, just before serving. Serve in heated bowls.

corned beef, barley, and cabbage soup

You don't have to be Irish to like this full-bodied soup. Corned beef and cabbage are a traditional pairing, and the addition of barley supplies extra flavor and texture. Corned beef is beef that has been cured in a seasoned brine (salt-and-water solution). The word corned derives from the English use of the word "corn" to describe a small particle, such as a grain of salt. Try serving this soup with the Rye Rusks on page 184.

MAKES 8 SERVINGS

1¼ pounds corned beef brisket

1 gallon Chicken Broth (page 16)

1½ onions, diced (about 2 cups)

½ head savoy cabbage, diced (about 6½ cups)

1 celery stalk, diced (about ¼ cup)

¼ cup pearl barley

Sachet: 3 crushed garlic cloves, 3 parsley stems, 1 bay leaf, 1 teaspoon dried thyme, and 1 teaspoon cracked black peppercorns enclosed in a large teaball or tied in a cheesecloth pouch

2 tomatoes, peeled, seeded, and diced (about 1¼ cups)

⅓ cup coarsely chopped flat-leaf parsley

Salt, to taste

Combine the brisket and broth in a soup pot. Bring to a simmer and cook until the meat is fork-tender, about 2 hours. If necessary, turn the meat occasionally during simmering to keep all surfaces moist.

Add the onions, cabbage, celery, barley, and sachet. Continue to simmer, 1 hour.

Remove the brisket and let cool slightly. Trim any excess fat and dice the meat.

Use a shallow spoon to skim any excess fat from the surface of the soup. Add the tomatoes and parsley. Simmer, 15 minutes.

Add the diced meat to the soup. Season with salt. Serve in heated bowls.

curried eggplant-and-lentil soup

The combination of eggplant, lentils, curry, and lemon is subtle, yet complex and exotic. Curry powder is a blend of up to twenty different ground ingredients. In India, where the exact ingredients vary from region to region, and even from cook to cook, it is usually ground fresh daily. Commercial curry powders bear little resemblance to fresh-ground versions, but they are perfectly adequate for this soup. Choose either a mild curry powder or the slightly hotter Madras curry powder. Cooking curry powder in fat before introducing liquid, as is done here, allows the fat to open up the fat-soluble flavor compounds in the curry powder, resulting in a more flavorful soup.

MAKES 8 SERVINGS

2 quarts Chicken or Vegetable Broth (pages 16, 20)

1 cup green or yellow lentils

4 waxy yellow potatoes, such as Yukon Gold or Yellow Finn

1 cup heavy cream

Salt, to taste

Freshly ground black pepper, to taste

3 tablespoons olive oil

2 medium eggplant (about 1 pound each), peeled and diced

1 onion, finely diced (about 1¼ cups)

1 garlic clove, minced (about ½ teaspoon)

2 tablespoons curry powder, or to taste

¼ cup fresh lemon juice

¼ cup chopped parsley

Simmer the broth, lentils, and potatoes in a soup pot until tender, about 45 minutes.

Strain the soup, reserving the liquid. Puree the solids and return to the soup pot. Add the cream and enough of the reserved liquid to achieve a thick soup consistency. Blend well. Season with the salt and pepper. Keep warm.

Heat the oil in a skillet over medium heat. Add the eggplant, onion, and garlic. Cook, 5 minutes, stirring occasionally. Stir in the curry powder and cook, 1 minute. Add the lemon juice and simmer gently until the eggplant is tender and the lemon juice has evaporated, 2–3 minutes. Season with salt and pepper.

Add the eggplant mixture to the soup and simmer, 5–10 minutes, to blend the flavors. Stir in the parsley. Serve in heated bowls.

mulligatawny soup

Mulligatawny soup is a product of the raj, *the British colonization of India. The British required a separate soup course with their meals, but the Indian custom was to serve all the foods in a meal at one time. Furthermore, the closest dishes to soup in Indian cuisine at that time were used as thin sauces poured over rice or dry curries, and were never drunk by themselves. Mulligatawny was born of this need. The name, which is a corruption of* milagu-tannir, *comes from the Tamil people of southern India. It means "pepper water," hence the large amount of black pepper in the recipe. For the best flavor, grind the spices fresh yourself. If you like, you can substitute chicken for the lamb without sacrificing authenticity.*

MAKES 8 SERVINGS

1–2 jalapeño peppers

4 teaspoons freshly ground black pepper

1 tablespoon ground coriander

2 teaspoons ground turmeric

³/₄ teaspoon ground cumin

¹/₂ teaspoon ground nutmeg

¹/₄ teaspoon ground cloves

5 garlic cloves

2 teaspoons grated or minced fresh ginger root

2 tablespoons butter

2 onions, diced (about 2¹/₂ cups)

1 pound lamb stew meat, cut into ¹/₂-inch cubes

2 quarts Chicken Broth (page 16)

¹/₃ cup tomato paste (about 3 ounces)

1¹/₂ teaspoons salt

2 carrots, diced (about ²/₃ cup)

2 apples, peeled, cored, and diced (about 1¹/₂ cups)

1 small potato, peeled and diced (about ³/₄ cup)

¹/₂ cup frozen peas

Lemon slices, optional

Remove the stems from the jalapeños. If you prefer a milder dish, remove the seeds as well. Grind the jalapeños, black pepper, coriander, turmeric, cumin, nutmeg, cloves, garlic, and ginger to a paste in a blender or mortar and pestle.

Heat the butter in a soup pot over medium heat. Cook the onion, stirring occasionally, until golden brown, about 10 minutes. Add the spice paste and cubed lamb and cook, 5 minutes.

Add the broth, tomato paste, and salt. Bring to a simmer and cook, 20 minutes.

Add the carrots, apples and potatoes. Continue to simmer the soup until everything is tender, about 20 more minutes.

Add the peas and simmer just until heated through, about 5 minutes. Serve the soup in heated bowls, garnished with lemon slices, if using.

leblebi (tunisian chickpea soup)

Chickpeas (garbanzo beans) are an important food in many parts of the world, particularly the band of countries that stretches from India through the Middle East to the Mediterranean. Buy dried chickpeas from a store that is likely to turn over its stock quickly, because chickpeas that are extremely dry will not soften properly no matter how long you cook them. Middle Eastern or Indian groceries and health-food stores are good bets. You can also substitute $3^{1}/_{2}$ cups drained and rinsed canned chickpeas for the dried, adding them with the spice paste.

MAKES 6 SERVINGS

$1^{1}/_{2}$ cups dried chickpeas, soaked overnight in 1 quart water

2 tablespoons olive oil

1 medium onion, diced

8 cups Chicken or Vegetable Broth (pages 16, 20)

1 teaspoon toasted cumin seeds

$^{1}/_{2}$ teaspoon salt, plus more to taste

5 garlic cloves, coarsely chopped

1 teaspoon Harissa (page 199)

Freshly ground black pepper, to taste

GARNISHES:

Three 1-inch-thick slices day old French bread, cut into 1-inch cubes

2 hard-boiled eggs, coarsely chopped

2 lemons, quartered

One 6-ounce can tuna, drained and flaked

$^{1}/_{2}$ cup thinly sliced scallion (white and green parts)

$^{1}/_{2}$ cup coarsely chopped capers, drained

$^{1}/_{3}$ cup Harissa (page 199)

Ground cumin, to taste

Extra-virgin olive oil, for serving

Heat the oil in a skillet over medium heat. Add the onion and cook until translucent, 6–8 minutes. Set aside.

Drain the chickpeas and place them in a large saucepan or a soup pot. Add the broth and bring to a simmer. Cover and simmer gently for 20 minutes.

Crush the whole cumin seeds with the $^{1}/_{2}$ teaspoon salt in a mortar. Add the garlic and crush to a paste. If you don't have a mortar and pestle, mince the garlic by hand, sprinkle it with the salt, and mash it to a paste with the side of a large knife. Use a spice grinder to grind the cumin seeds, or you can substitute $^{1}/_{2}$ teaspoon toasted ground cumin. Add the garlic-spice paste and harissa to the soup. Continue to simmer until the chickpeas are barely tender, 15–20 minutes.

Add the onions and the olive oil they were cooked in, and simmer until the chickpeas are completely tender, about 15 minutes. Season with salt and pepper.

To serve, place the bread chunks in heated soup bowls and ladle about $^{1}/_{2}$ cup of broth into each bowl. Offer the remaining garnishes in small bowls or on a tray, along with the olive oil and additional salt and pepper. Once the bread has softened, add the chickpeas to the soup bowls. Serve immediately.

hlelem (tunisian vegetable-and-bean soup)

Packed with beans and greens, this slightly spicy vegetable soup is both tasty and good for you. Harissa is a Tunisian hot sauce or paste usually made with hot chiles, garlic, cumin, coriander, caraway, and olive oil. It's available in cans, jars, or tubes from Middle Eastern markets and specialty stores. Or, make your own (page 199).

MAKES 8 SERVINGS

3 ounces dried lima or butter beans (about ½ cup)

3 ounces dried chickpeas (about ½ cup)

2 tablespoons olive oil

2 garlic cloves, minced (about 1 teaspoon)

1 celery stalk, large outer veins trimmed, diced (about ½ cup)

½ onion, minced (about ¾ cup)

1 quart Chicken Broth (page 16)

⅓ cup tomato paste (about 3 ounces)

4 large Swiss chard leaves, stems removed and cut into 1-inch pieces, leaves shredded (about 5½ ounces)

1½ ounces angel hair pasta, broken into bite-sized pieces (about ⅓ cup)

2 tablespoons Harissa (page 199)

Salt, to taste

Freshly ground black pepper, to taste

½ cup chopped parsley

Soak the dried lima beans and the chickpeas separately, overnight, in 3 times their volume of water. Drain and cook separately in 2 times their volume of fresh water until tender, about 45 minutes. Drain and reserve the cooking water from both the lima beans and the chickpeas; combine the cooking liquids and set aside. Combine the lima beans and chickpeas; set aside.

Heat the olive oil in a soup pot over medium heat. Add the garlic, celery, and onion. Cook, stirring occasionally, until the onion is translucent, 4–6 minutes.

Add the broth, the reserved cooking liquid from the beans, and the tomato paste. Mix until well blended, and bring to a simmer, 10 minutes.

Approximately 10 minutes before serving, add the cooked beans and chick peas, Swiss chard, and pasta. Simmer until the pasta and chard stems are tender, about 10 minutes.

Add the harissa and stir until blended. Season with salt and pepper. Serve in heated bowls, garnished with chopped parsley.

french lentil soup

The earthy flavor of lentils is brightened by Riesling and sherry wine vinegar in this refined lentil soup. It is a brothy soup but, if you'd like it to be thicker, you can puree half and combine it with the unpureed half. If you store this soup in the refrigerator, it may become thicker. Adjust the consistency as necessary by adding more broth, and be sure to check the seasoning.

MAKES 8 SERVINGS

2 tablespoons vegetable oil

1 onion, finely diced (about 1¼ cups)

1 garlic clove, minced (about ½ teaspoon)

2 carrots, finely diced (about ⅔ cup)

1 leek, white and light green parts, finely diced (about 1¼ cups)

1 celery stalk, finely diced (about ½ cup)

1 tablespoon tomato paste

7 cups Chicken or Vegetable Broth (pages 16, 20)

1¾ cups French (green) lentils (about 10 ounces)

¼ cup Riesling or other slightly sweet white wine

2 tablespoons sherry wine vinegar

½ lemon

Sachet: 2 sprigs fresh or 1 teaspoon dried thyme, 1 bay leaf, and ¼ teaspoon caraway seeds enclosed in a large teaball or tied in a cheesecloth pouch

½ teaspoon salt, or to taste

¼ teaspoon freshly ground white pepper, or to taste

Heat the oil in a soup pot over medium heat. Add the onion and garlic. Cook, stirring occasionally, until the onion is translucent, 4–6 minutes.

Add the carrots, leek, and celery. Cook, stirring occasionally until softened, 5–7 minutes.

Add the tomato paste, stir well, and cook, 2 minutes.

Add the remaining ingredients and bring to a simmer. Cook until the lentils are tender, about 40 minutes. Remove and discard the sachet and lemon half.

Season with salt and pepper. Serve in heated bowls.

red lentil soup

Of all vegetables, lentils, at approximately twenty-five percent, are second only to soybeans in protein content. They have been culti-vated by humans for millennia, as evidenced by their presence at ancient Egyptian and prehistoric European sites. Today, lentils are available in several varieties, such as the yellow lentil and the green (French) lentil. The red (Egyptian) lentil is the quickest cooking of all lentils, and lends itself well to soup making because, as it cooks, it tends to fall apart and practically purees itself.

MAKES 8 SERVINGS

3 tablespoons unsalted butter

1/2 large onion, minced (about 1 cup)

2 garlic cloves, minced (about 1 teaspoon)

1/2 celery stalk, diced (about 1/4 cup)

1 pound red lentils

1 teaspoon ground cumin

2 tablespoons long-grain white rice

2 1/2 quarts Chicken Broth, or as needed (page 16)

Juice of 1/2 lemon

Salt, to taste

Freshly ground white pepper, to taste

Melt the butter in a soup pot over medium heat and add the garlic, onion, and celery. Cook until the onion is translucent, 4–6 minutes.

Reduce the heat to low, add the lentils and cumin, and stir to coat evenly with butter. Cook, 4–5 minutes.

Add the rice and 5 cups of the chicken broth. Bring to a simmer and cook, stirring often to avoid scorching, until the lentils dissolve and begin to look like a pureed soup, 30–45 minutes. Add the remaining broth as needed to adjust the consistency. Heat through.

Season with the lemon juice, salt, and pepper. Serve in heated bowls.

shrimp and andouille gumbo

The secret of success for gumbo is to cook the roux *(the flour-and-oil paste) until it is very dark. You want to stop just short of burning it. Be very careful when making the roux; it will get extremely hot and may bubble and sputter. If any of it hits your skin, it will stick and burn, which is why dark roux is sometimes known by another name: Cajun napalm. For information on filé powder, see page 83.*

MAKES 8 SERVINGS

¹/₄ cup vegetable oil

¹/₄ cup all-purpose flour

2 quarts Chicken Broth (page 16)

2 bay leaves

¹/₂ pound shrimp, peeled, deveined, and diced

¹/₄ pound andouille sausage, diced (about 1 link)

¹/₂ pound fresh okra, trimmed, sliced ¹/₄-inch thick

Salt, to taste

¹/₂ teaspoon cayenne pepper, or to taste

¹/₄ teaspoon freshly ground black pepper, or to taste

Tabasco sauce, to taste

2 teaspoons filé powder, optional

4 cups boiled white rice, optional

Heat the oil in a soup pot over high heat. Reduce heat to medium-low, add the flour, and cook, stirring frequently, until the flour turns dark brown and has an intensely nutty aroma, 10–15 minutes.

Add the broth gradually, whisking well to work out any lumps. Simmer, 15–20 minutes, stirring frequently.

Add the bay leaves, diced shrimp, sausage, and okra to the soup and cook until the okra is tender, about 15 minutes.

Remove and discard the bay leaves. Season with the salt, cayenne, black pepper, and Tabasco.

Remove the soup from the heat, and gradually add the filé powder, if using. Serve in heated bowls, ladled over rice, if using.

FACING PAGE: Preparing a dark roux (top left); adding broth gradually (top right); stirring the simmering soup (bottom left); finishing with filé powder off the heat (bottom right)

seafood gumbo

In addition to a small amount of roux, this gumbo is thickened with filé powder, which is the ground, dried leaves of the sassafras tree. It has a woodsy, root-beer-like flavor. Filé is usually added to gumbo after it is removed from the heat, because excessive heat can make it stringy. Some people do not care for the texture of filé, so you might prefer to serve it on the side and allow individuals to add it to their liking. You can find filé in the spice section of most large supermarkets. Incidentally, the vegetable combination of onion, celery, and green pepper is known as the "Cajun Trinity" because it is used extensively in Cajun cooking.

MAKES 8 SERVINGS

Seasoning Mix (see box)

1 tablespoon canola oil or unsalted butter

2 tablespoons all-purpose flour

1½ onions, diced (about 2½ cups)

3 celery stalks, diced (about 1½ cups)

1 small green pepper, diced (about ¾ cup)

1 garlic clove, minced

¾ teaspoon Tabasco sauce

1 cup tomato sauce

3½ cups Fish Broth (page 19)

1 link andouille sausage, sliced

8 fresh oysters, shucked

3 plum tomatoes, peeled, seeded, and diced (about ¾ cup)

¾ cup crabmeat, picked over for shells

⅔ cup small shrimp, peeled and deveined

⅔ cup cooked white rice (⅓ cup uncooked)

1–2 teaspoons filé powder

Salt, to taste

Freshly ground black pepper, to taste

Combine the seasoning-mix ingredients. Set aside.

Heat the oil in a soup pot over low heat. Add the flour and cook, stirring frequently, until the flour turns dark brown and has an intensely nutty aroma, about 10 minutes.

Increase the heat to high and add the onion, celery, and green pepper. Cook until the vegetables are softened, about 5 minutes.

Add the garlic, Tabasco, and seasoning mix. Stir well and cook, 1 minute.

Stir in the tomato sauce and bring to a simmer. Cook, 10 minutes.

Add the broth, return to a simmer, and cook, 45 minutes.

Meanwhile, cook the sausage in a nonstick skillet over medium heat until browned on both sides, 5–7 minutes. Drain on paper towels.

Add the sausage, oysters, tomatoes, crab, shrimp, and rice to the gumbo. Bring to a boil, stir in the filé, cover, remove from the heat, and let stand 10–12 minutes.

Season with salt and pepper. Serve in heated bowls.

SEASONING MIX:

¼ teaspoon garlic powder

¼ teaspoon freshly ground white pepper

Pinch freshly ground black pepper

Pinch cayenne

Pinch hot paprika

Pinch dried thyme

Pinch dried oregano

callaloo

Callaloo is the greens of the taro root. It is popular in the Caribbean, where it is cooked and eaten in much the same way that collard or turnip greens are in the southeastern United States. It is also used to make a wonderful soup of the same name. Callaloo can be purchased at Caribbean markets but, if you cannot find it in your area, fresh spinach makes a fine substitute. Whatever greens you use, be sure to wash them thoroughly to remove any grit.

MAKES 8 SERVINGS

5 ounces slab bacon, rind removed, cut into small dice

1/2 onion, minced (about 3/4 cup)

2 garlic cloves, minced (about 1 teaspoon)

2 quarts Chicken Broth (page 16)

1 pound fresh okra, sliced 1/4-inch thick (about 4 cups)

1 1/2 cups coarsely chopped callaloo (about 10 ounces)

1 Scotch bonnet chile, pricked with a fork and left whole

4 teaspoons coarsely chopped fresh thyme leaves, or 2 teaspoons dried

Salt, to taste

Freshly ground black pepper, to taste

10 ounces crabmeat, picked over for shells

3 scallions, sliced

3/4 cup coconut milk

Juice of 2 limes, or more, to taste

Cook the bacon in a soup pot over medium heat until crisp, about 8 minutes. Add the onion and garlic and cook, stirring occasionally, until softened, about 3 minutes.

Add the broth, okra, greens, chile, and thyme along with a pinch of salt and pepper. Bring to a simmer and cook, 30 minutes.

Just before serving, remove the chile and add the crabmeat, scallions, coconut milk, and lime juice. Season with salt and pepper. Serve in heated bowls.

cream soups

A CCORDING TO CLASSIC DEFINITIONS, a cream soup is based on a *béchamel* sauce—milk thickened with roux—and is finished with heavy cream. A *velouté* soup is based on a light velouté sauce—a broth thickened with roux— and is finished with a *liaison* of heavy cream and egg yolks. Contemporary chefs no longer draw a distinction between the two and, in modern kitchens, frequently substitute a velouté base for the béchamel in cream soups. True velouté soups, like the Waterzooi on page 107, are less frequently prepared today than they once were, because the addition of a liaison shortens the shelf life of the soup. Furthermore, soups finished with a liaison are very rich and high in calories.

These days, a cream soup is generally made by simmering the major flavoring ingredient in thickened broth until tender. The solids are strained out and, in most cases, pureed and returned to the soup. A second straining is then often suggested to develop the velvety-smooth texture associated with excellent cream soups.

MAIN INGREDIENTS FOR CREAM SOUPS

Most cream soups are based on a full-bodied broth thickened with *roux,* a combination of flour and fat. In some cases, milk is the base liquid. In other cases, potatoes or rice might be used as the thickener instead of roux.

Cream soups based on chicken or fish are typically made from double broths. The poultry or fish used to make the double broth is then usually added as a garnish at the end of cooking time, or just before the soup is served.

Trim, peel, and cut vegetables for cream soups according to type and recipe requirements. It is less important that the cuts be as neat and uniform for cream soups as for hearty soups because they are going to be pureed. However, it is still important that the cuts be small and relatively uniform in size, so that they will cook evenly.

SUPPORTING FLAVORS

Aromatic vegetables (carrots, onions, celery, etc.) should be cut relatively small to allow their flavors to be released properly. If a very white or ivory cream soup is desired, use a combination of parsnips, leeks, and celery. Other aromatic combinations, including sachets of various herbs and spices, are also used in some cream soups.

Finishing ingredients, final flavoring and seasonings, and garnishes should be assembled and ready to add just before serving. Fresh sweet cream is the most common finishing ingredient, but liaisons and flavored creams (scented with ginger or other aromatics) may also be used. Garnishes for cream soup are usually a diced meat or vegetable that reflects the major flavoring ingredient. For example, cream of broccoli soup is typically garnished with cooked broccoli florets. If you plan to store the soup and serve it later, do not add these ingredients until just before you intend to serve the soup.

EVALUATING THE QUALITY OF CREAM SOUPS

Cream soups should have a velvety mouthfeel with a body, consistency, and texture similar to cold heavy cream—perfectly smooth and somewhat thick. The flavor should be that of the major flavoring ingredient, and it should not taste too strongly of heavy cream. The color will vary, depending upon the major flavoring ingredient but, in all cases, it will be relatively pale.

Cream soups are prone to several problems that can occur during preparation or storage. They are discussed here.

- *Consistency too thick.* Cream soups may become too thick during cooking and storage. The soup can be thinned with broth until the desired consistency is achieved. Do not thin cream soups with more heavy cream, it can mask the main flavor.

- *Consistency too thin.* Either too much broth or not enough roux was used to prepare the soup base.

- *Sour or off flavors.* These soups have a brief shelf life once the cream has been added. To extend storage time, be sure that the base is properly chilled and stored, then finish only the amount needed at a time. Check cream soups carefully for any souring or off odors. Once a soup begins to curdle or taste sour, it cannot be salvaged.

- *Starchy taste.* The cooking time is important. The soup must be simmered long enough to cook out the raw flour taste from the roux.

- *Scorched taste.* Using moderate cooking heat, heavy-gauge pots, and stirring cream soups as they cook, will prevent scorching and promote the development of a clear flavor.

1.

2.

3.

4.

basic cream soup method

 Cook the vegetables in fat.

In addition to the supporting vegetables, you may also need to cook various other vegetables that will act as the major flavoring of the soup, such as broccoli, mushrooms, or tomatoes (fig. 1). This should be done gently, over low heat, in oil or butter, until the vegetables begin to release their juices.

Be careful not to undercook the vegetables, because this step is of great importance in determining the quality of the finished soup (fig. 2). On the other hand, avoid cooking them until they become even lightly browned. They should stay light in color, cooking just until tender and translucent.

 Stir in the flour.

Sprinkle the flour into the pot as you stir (fig. 3). Once the flour is added, continue cooking and stirring for a few minutes to distribute the flour evenly, and to begin the process of cooking out the raw taste of the flour (fig. 4).

Add the liquid and bring it to a simmer.

Slowly add the liquid to the pot, while you stir or whisk constantly to prevent any lumps of flour from forming (fig. 5). Bring the soup just to a simmer, over low heat. Stir frequently to prevent scorching.

Simmer until the vegetables are very tender.

Skim the surface as often as needed during the cooking time to remove any impurities that could affect the finished soup's flavor. Pulling the pot slightly to the side of the burner will cause the foam to collect on one side of the pot, where it can be more easily skimmed away.

Stir frequently to prevent scorching (fig. 6). If there is a slight hint of sticking or scorching, immediately transfer the soup to a cool, clean pot. Check for any scorched taste. If there is none, you can continue cooking the soup. However, if the soup has a burnt aroma or flavor, it is generally beyond repair.

5.

Add any additional ingredients at appropriate intervals. The time at which certain ingredients are added to the soup will depend upon their individual cooking requirements. Tender new peas will become gray and pasty if allowed to cook too long. A sachet left in the soup too long may lose its fresh flavor. Consult individual recipes for specific instructions on when to add ingredients.

Taste the soup often as it develops. You can remove the soup from the heat once all of its ingredients are very tender and the soup has a good flavor.

Strain and puree the solids.

6.

Some soups are just strained once, to remove all the solids. For others, like vegetable cream soups, the solids are usually pureed and combined with enough soup liquid to achieve the proper consistency, which should be similar to the consistency of cold heavy cream. The liquid should be gradually added to the puree, until just enough has been added to reach the desired consistency and flavor (fig. 7). Occasionally, evaporation during cooking may cause your soup to be too thick, even after you have added all the soup liquid. In this case, add more broth or water to thin the soup to the desired consistency.

For the smoothest consistency, the soup can then be strained again through a fine sieve. At this point, the soup can be properly cooled and stored as outlined in chapter 1, or it can be finished and served.

Add the finishing ingredients.

7.

To finish a hot soup with cream, bring the cream to a simmer, then add it to the soup (fig. 8). To finish with a liaison, see the instructions (page 97). In both cases, do not allow the soup to boil after the finishing ingredient has been added or it might curdle.

Remember that the right amount of cream or liaison will produce a soup that is delicately flavored, suave, and perfectly smooth, but too much cream will detract from the major flavor of the soup, masking the original taste.

Make any additional adjustments to the soup's consistency or flavor once the cream has been added. If necessary, reheat the garnish and either add it directly to the soup, or garnish individual portions.

8.

cream of broccoli soup

This velvety soup is the essence of broccoli. It's relatively simple to make, yet is very elegant and refined—try serving this soup as a first course for company. Best of all, this one recipe provides a blueprint for creating elegant cream soups from any seasonal fresh vegetables.

MAKES 8 SERVINGS

2 pounds broccoli

¼ cup vegetable or olive oil

1 medium onion, chopped (about 1¼ cups)

1 celery stalk, chopped (about ½ cup)

1 leek, white and light green parts, chopped (about 1¼ cups)

¼ cup all-purpose flour

1½ quarts Chicken Broth (page 16)

½ cup heavy cream, heated

Fresh lemon juice, to taste

Salt, to taste

Freshly ground black pepper, to taste

Separate the broccoli into stems and florets. Trim away the tough outer parts of the stems. Set aside 1 cup of the nicest-looking small florets. Coarsely chop the remaining broccoli florets and stems.

Heat the oil in a soup pot over medium heat. Add the onion, celery, leek, and chopped broccoli. Cook, stirring frequently, until the onion is translucent, 6–8 minutes.

Add the flour and stir well to combine. Cook, stirring frequently, 4 minutes.

Add broth to the pot gradually, whisking to work out any lumps of flour. Bring the soup to a simmer and cook, 45 minutes. Stir frequently and skim as needed.

Strain the solids, reserving the liquid. Puree the solids, adding liquid as necessary to facilitate pureeing.

Combine the puree with enough reserved liquid to achieve the consistency of heavy cream. Strain the soup through a fine sieve (optional). Return the soup to a simmer.

Meanwhile, steam or boil the reserved broccoli florets until just tender.

Remove the soup from the heat and add heated cream. Season with lemon juice, salt, and pepper. Serve in heated bowls, garnished with florets.

CREAM OF ASPARAGUS

Replace the broccoli with 3 pounds asparagus. Reserve 16 of the nicest-looking asparagus tips for the garnish, and coarsely chop the remaining asparagus.

CREAM OF CELERY

Replace the broccoli with an equal weight of celery or celeriac. Garnish with diced cooked celery.

cream of tomato soup

This soup vies with chicken noodle for the title of ultimate comfort soup. It's full of tomato flavor and tastes much better than the version that many of us grew up on—the one that comes in a red-and-white can. If you have really flavorful, ripe tomatoes, use them in place of the canned tomatoes. Otherwise, canned tomatoes offer the best flavor and consistency.

MAKES 8 SERVINGS

3 tablespoons vegetable oil

2 carrots, diced (about 2/3 cup)

2 celery stalks, diced (about 1 cup)

1 small onion, diced (about 3/4 cup)

1 garlic clove, minced (about 1/2 teaspoon)

1/2 cup all-purpose flour

1 quart Chicken Broth (page 16), plus more as needed

2 1/3 cups drained, canned plum tomatoes, chopped

2 cups tomato puree

1/4 teaspoon freshly ground black pepper, or to taste

2 parsley stems

1/2 bay leaf

1 cup light cream, hot

Salt, to taste

Heat the oil in a soup pot over medium heat. Add the carrots, celery, onion, and garlic. Cook, stirring occasionally, until softened, 6–8 minutes.

Add the flour and blend well. Continue to cook, stirring frequently, 3–4 minutes.

Add the broth and blend well. Add the chopped tomatoes, tomato puree, and pepper. Bring to a simmer and cook, 30 minutes. Add the parsley stems and bay leaf and continue to simmer, 30 minutes.

Pass the soup through a strainer, pressing hard on the solids to recover as much liquid as possible.

Blend the hot cream into the strained soup. Adjust the consistency with more broth, if necessary. Season with salt and more pepper, if desired. Serve in heated bowls.

watercress soup

This thick, rich soup is tangy with the flavors of watercress and sour cream. Watercress grows wild in streams and brooks, but can also be found in most supermarkets, sold in bunches or bags. Look for fresh, firm leaves with no sign of yellowing. Store in the refrigerator stems down in a container of water covered with a plastic bag (this storage method works well for other leafy herbs, like parsley and cilantro).

MAKES 8 SERVINGS

4 cups watercress, rinsed

2 tablespoons unsalted butter

1 leek, white and light green part, chopped (about 1¼ cups)

1 small onion, chopped (about 1 cup)

1 quart Chicken Broth (page 16)

1¼ pounds yellow or white potatoes, thinly sliced (about 3 potatoes)

½ teaspoon salt, or to taste

¼ teaspoon freshly ground white pepper, or to taste

1 cup sour cream

Bring a large pot of water to a boil. Reserve 8 of the nicest-looking watercress sprigs for garnish. Remove the stems from the remaining watercress and add the leaves to the boiling water. Boil until just wilted. Drain and squeeze out any excess moisture. Puree the watercress and set aside.

Heat the butter in a soup pot over medium heat. Add the leek and onions. Cook, stirring occasionally, until the onion is translucent, about 7 minutes.

Add the broth and bring it to a simmer. Add the potatoes and simmer until tender, about 25 minutes.

Puree the soup. Add the watercress puree. Return to a simmer.

Stir in the sour cream and heat through. Do not allow the soup to reach a simmer again. Season with salt and pepper. Serve in heated bowls, garnished with watercress sprigs.

cream of mushroom soup

So-called exotic varieties of mushrooms, such as cremini and oyster, work well in this soup, as do regular white mushrooms. Use a combination or a single variety, depending on your taste and what's available. You may also opt to season the soup with a touch of sherry, instead of lemon juice. For an extra special presentation, ladle the soup into ovenproof bowls. Top the bowls with puff pastry cut to fit the bowls, seal the edges with some beaten egg, and bake until golden, according to package directions.

MAKES 8 SERVINGS

7 tablespoons unsalted butter, divided

8 cups chopped mushrooms (about 1¼ pounds)

2 celery stalks, finely chopped (about 1 cup)

1 leek, white part only, thinly sliced (about 1¼ cups)

½ cup all-purpose flour

5 cups Chicken Broth (page 16)

1 fresh thyme sprig

1 cup sliced mushrooms (about 2½ ounces)

1½ cups heavy cream, heated

Fresh lemon juice, to taste

Salt, to taste

Freshly ground white pepper, to taste

Melt 6 tablespoons of the butter in a soup pot over medium heat. Add the chopped mushrooms, celery, and leek. Cook, stirring frequently, until softened, 6–8 minutes.

Add the flour and cook, stirring constantly, 3–4 minutes.

Whisk in the broth gradually. Add the thyme sprig, bring to a simmer, and cook, 30 minutes.

Meanwhile, melt the remaining butter in a skillet. Add the sliced mushrooms and sauté until cooked through, about 5 minutes. Remove from the heat.

Remove the thyme and discard. Puree the soup, then strain through cheesecloth or a fine sieve. Return the soup to the soup pot and place over low heat. Add the heavy cream and season with the lemon juice, salt, and pepper. Heat the soup, but do not let it boil.

Serve in heated bowls, garnished with the cooked, sliced mushrooms.

roasted red pepper, leek, and potato cream soup

This silky-smooth cream soup derives its thickness and most of its texture from potatoes, rather than from a roux. The sweetness of the leek and red peppers make a wonderful combination. If you wish, substitute 1 cup drained, bottled, roasted red peppers for the freshly roasted peppers.

MAKES 8 SERVINGS

2 red bell peppers

4 tablespoons unsalted butter

3 cups diced leeks
(white and light green parts from 2–3 leeks)

4 medium russet potatoes, peeled and diced
(about 8 cups)

6 cups Chicken Broth (page 16)

1 sprig fresh or ½ teaspoon dried thyme, enclosed
in a large teaball or tied in a cheesecloth pouch

1 cup heavy cream or half-and-half, heated

Salt, to taste

Freshly ground white pepper, to taste

½ cup finely sliced scallion, green part only,
or chives

Preheat the broiler. Place the red peppers under the broiler, turning them as they roast, so that they blacken evenly on all sides. Put the peppers in a small bowl and cover, letting them steam, 10 minutes, then remove them from the bowl and pull off the skins. Use the back of a knife to scrape away any bits that don't come away easily. Remove the seeds, ribs, and stems. Chop the flesh coarsely.

Melt the butter in a soup pot over medium heat. Add the roasted peppers and leeks. Stir to coat well. Reduce the heat to low, cover the pot, and cook until the leeks are tender and translucent, 5–7 minutes.

Add the potatoes, broth, and thyme. Bring to a simmer and cook, partially covered, until the potatoes are soft enough to mash, 25–30 minutes. During cooking, skim and discard any foam that rises to the surface. Keep the liquid level constant by adding additional broth as necessary.

Remove the thyme and discard. Strain the solids, reserving the liquid. Puree the solids with a small amount of the liquid. Return the puree to the remaining liquid and strain through a fine sieve.

Bring the soup back to a simmer. Remove from the heat and add the heated cream. Season with salt and pepper. Serve in heated bowls, garnished with scallions or chives.

billi bi (cream of mussel soup)

There are several stories surrounding the origin of this suave French soup, the most popular being that a chef at the famed Maxim's of Paris named it after American tin tycoon William B. (Billy B.) Leeds, a regular customer and huge fan of this soup. Don't pull the beards from the mussels until you are ready to cook them, as this kills the mussels. A mussel's shell should close if it is tapped on a counter. Any mussels that do not close, or that are filled with mud (they will make a dull sound when tapped), should be discarded.

MAKES 6 TO 8 SERVINGS

2 pounds mussels

1 tablespoon minced shallots

1 cup white wine

1 teaspoon saffron threads

4 tablespoons butter

1 onion, minced

5 tablespoons flour

5 cups Fish Broth (page 19)

Sachet: 5–6 parsley stems, 6–8 black peppercorns, 1 sprig fresh or ½ teaspoon dried thyme, and 1 bay leaf enclosed in a large teaball or tied in a cheesecloth pouch

1 egg yolk

1 cup heavy cream or half-and-half

Salt, to taste

Freshly ground white pepper, to taste

Pull the beards from the mussels. Scrub the mussels well under cold running water. Set aside.

Combine the shallots, wine, and saffron threads in a pot large enough to hold the mussels. Place over medium-high heat and bring to a boil. Add the mussels, cover the pot tightly, and reduce the heat to medium-low. Cook the mussels for 5–6 minutes, shaking the pot occasionally. Remove the mussels from the pot as their shells open. Remove the meat from the shells; refrigerate. Strain the cooking liquid and reserve.

Heat the butter in a 3-quart pot over medium heat. Add the onion and stir to coat evenly. Cover the pot and cook the onion until translucent, 3–4 minutes. Add the flour and cook, 3–4 minutes, stirring almost constantly with a wooden spoon.

Gradually add the mussel cooking liquid and fish broth, using a whisk to work out any lumps after each addition. Add the sachet and bring to a simmer. Simmer gently, 45 minutes, stirring occasionally and skimming as necessary.

Discard the sachet. Strain the soup through cheesecloth or a fine sieve. Return the soup to the stove and bring to a simmer.

Make a liaison by blending the egg yolk with the cream in a bowl. Stir in about 1 cup of the hot soup, then stir the heated liaison mixture into the soup. Simmer, 3 minutes.

Add the mussel meat to the soup and simmer until the mussels are heated through. Adjust the seasoning. Serve in heated bowls.

oyster and fennel soup

The flavors of fennel and oyster pair beautifully in this soup. Each shines through without overpowering the other. If your grocery only sells fennel with the tops removed, look for bulbs that are firm, unblemished, and heavy for their size. You may substitute fresh dill for the fennel leaf garnish suggested here.

MAKES 8 SERVINGS

1 fennel bulb, preferably with tops still intact

1 quart Chicken Broth (page 16)

1 pint Fish Broth (page 19)

2 tablespoons unsalted butter

1 leek, white part only, diced (about 1 cup)

22 fresh oysters, shucked, juices reserved, divided

6 white or yellow potatoes, peeled and diced (about 6 cups)

¼ cup white wine

2 teaspoons fresh thyme leaves, chopped

½ tablespoon fennel seeds, toasted and crushed

1 cup heavy cream, heated

1 cup milk, heated

Salt, to taste

Freshly ground white pepper, to taste

Cut the tops from the fennel bulb. Chop 2 tablespoons of the feathery leaves, and set aside for a garnish. Chop the remaining stems and leaves. Core and dice the bulb. Reserve.

Bring the chicken and fish broths to a simmer in a large saucepan. Add the chopped fennel stems and leaves. Simmer, 20 minutes, then strain and reserve the broth. Discard the fennel stems and leaves.

Heat the butter in a soup pot over medium heat. Add the diced fennel bulb and leek. Cook, stirring occasionally, until softened, 5–7 minutes.

Add the fennel broth, 6 of the oysters, and the potatoes, white wine, thyme, and fennel seeds. Bring to a simmer and cook until the potatoes are tender, about 25 minutes.

Puree the soup. Strain through a fine sieve or cheesecloth-lined colander for an extra-smooth consistency, optional.

Return the soup to a simmer. Remove from the heat and add the remaining oysters with their juices, the chopped fennel leaves, and the hot cream and milk. Season with salt and pepper. Serve in heated bowls.

cheddar cheese soup

This soup does not have any cream in it, but the cheese makes it plenty rich. If you make this soup in advance, reheat it in a double boiler over simmering water, or in a microwave at medium power, so that the cheese doesn't separate from the soup, giving it a curdled appearance. Try other cheeses, such as Brie, Camembert, or even a mild goat cheese.

MAKES 6 SERVINGS

1/2 cup butter (1 stick)

2 leeks, white and light green parts, finely diced (about 2 1/2 cups)

1 onion, finely diced (about 1 1/4 cups)

1 celery stalk, finely diced (about 1/2 cup)

1/4 cup flour

2 teaspoons dry mustard

1 cup ale or white wine

6 cups Chicken or Vegetable Broth (pages 16, 20)

3 cups grated cheddar or Monterey jack cheese (about 1 pound)

Tabasco sauce, to taste

Salt, to taste

Freshly ground white pepper, to taste

1/4 cup finely diced canned green chiles

2 tablespoons minced cilantro or parsley

2 tablespoons finely diced pickled jalapeños, optional

Melt the butter in a soup pot over medium heat. Add the leeks, onion, and celery. Stir to coat. Cover the pot and cook until the vegetables are tender, 4–5 minutes.

Add the flour and stir well with a wooden spoon. Cook, 4–5 minutes, stirring almost constantly. Add the dry mustard and ale, stirring to make a thick paste. Add the broth in batches, using a whisk to work out any lumps between each addition.

Bring the soup to a simmer and continue to simmer gently, 1 hour. Stir the soup occasionally, and skim as necessary.

Strain the soup through a sieve, reserving the liquid. Puree the solids and return to the soup pot. Add enough of the reserved liquid to achieve a soup consistency and strain once more.

Return the soup to a simmer. Whisk in the cheese and simmer until the cheese melts, about 1 minute. Season with the Tabasco sauce, salt, and white pepper. Serve in heated bowls, garnished with chiles, cilantro, and jalapeños if using.

chestnut soup with fresh ginger

Chestnuts were an important part of the Native American diet, furnishing an excellent source of protein and carbohydrate. Today, chestnuts are favored not only for their wonderful flavor, but also for their low fat content, a rarity in all other nuts. Fresh chestnuts are generally available from September through February. Select firm nuts with unblemished shells and store in a cool, dry place.

MAKES 4 TO 6 SERVINGS

10 ounces chestnuts

1 tablespoon unsalted butter

1 celery stalk, diced (about ½ cup)

1 carrot, diced (about ⅓ cup)

1 leek, white and light green parts, chopped (about 1¼ cups)

½ onion, diced (about ¾ cup)

1 quart Chicken Broth (page 16)

2 tablespoons grated fresh ginger root

2 tablespoons freshly squeezed orange juice, or to taste

¾ cup heavy cream, heated

½ teaspoon salt, or to taste

¼ teaspoon freshly ground black pepper, or to taste

Preheat the oven to 400°F or bring a large pot of water to a rolling boil. Score an X on the flat side of each chestnut with the tip of a paring knife. Roast them on a baking sheet in the oven or boil them, until the outer skin begins to curl. Peel away both the outer and inner layers of skin. Chestnuts are easiest to peel while still warm; if you are experiencing difficulties, re-warm the nuts by dropping them back into the simmering water or re-turning them to the warm oven. Reserve 4–6 whole chestnuts to garnish each bowl of soup, if desired. Chop the remaining chestnuts and set aside.

Heat the butter in a soup pot over medium heat. Add the celery, carrot, leek, and onion. Cook, stirring frequently, until the onion is light golden brown, 8–10 minutes.

Add the broth, chopped chestnuts, and ginger. Bring the soup to a sim-mer and cook, stirring occasionally, until all of the ingredients are very tender, 35–40 minutes.

Puree the soup and return to medium heat. Add the orange juice and simmer, 2 minutes.

Add the cream to the soup. Season with salt, pepper, and more orange juice, if desired. Serve in heated bowls, garnished with whole chestnuts, if using.

serving suggestion

Instead of topping the soup with a whole roasted chestnut, whip a little heavy cream, fold in an equal amount of sour cream, add some grated fresh ginger root to taste, and place a spoonful of this ginger-scented cream on each serving.

sweet potato and peanut soup

Sweet potatoes are high in vitamins A and E, as well as being a good source of vitamin B$_6$ and potassium and iron. Here they combine with peanut butter and chopped peanuts to become a unique, slightly sweet soup. This soup will appeal to most adults, but it's also a great way to get kids who are picky eaters to eat a healthy vegetable.

MAKES 8 SERVINGS

3 tablespoons unsalted butter

1 celery stalk, coarsely chopped (about 1/2 cup)

1 onion, coarsely chopped (about 1 1/4 cups)

1 garlic clove, minced (about 1/2 teaspoon)

1/2 leek, white and light green parts, coarsely chopped (about 3/4 cup)

1 1/2 sweet potatoes, peeled and sliced 1/3-inch thick (about 3 cups)

1 quart Chicken Broth (page 16)

3 tablespoons creamy peanut butter

1/4 cinnamon stick

1 1/4 cups heavy cream, divided

Salt, to taste

2 tablespoons molasses

Freshly grated nutmeg, to taste

3/4 cup peanuts

Preheat the oven to 325°F. Melt the butter in a soup pot over medium heat. Add the celery, onion, garlic, and leek. Stir to coat. Cook, stirring frequently, until the vegetables are softened, 4–6 minutes.

Add the sweet potatoes, broth, peanut butter, and cinnamon stick. Bring to a simmer and cook until the potatoes are fully tender, about 25 minutes.

Meanwhile, spread the peanuts in a single layer in a pie pan. Toast the peanuts in the oven until light brown, 3–5 minutes. Shake the pan occasionally and watch carefully (nuts can burn quickly). Let the peanuts cool, chop coarsely, and set aside.

Remove the cinnamon stick and discard. Puree the soup and strain it. Return the soup to the soup pot and place over low heat. Add 1/2 cup of the cream. Season with salt. Keep warm, but do not boil.

Combine the remaining cream with the molasses, nutmeg, and a pinch of salt. Whip until stiff peaks form.

Serve the soup in heated bowls, garnished with the whipped cream and chopped nuts.

pumpkin soup with ginger cream

Look for plain pumpkin pieces in the frozen foods section of your market. Canned pumpkin will not work quite as well in this recipe, although it can be substituted if fresh or frozen pumpkin is unavailable. This soup may be garnished with a scattering of toasted pumpkin seeds. For an elegant presentation, add a tablespoon of diced, cooked lobster meat to each portion.

MAKES 8 SERVINGS

2 teaspoons butter

2 garlic cloves, minced (about 1 teaspoon)

1 onion, diced (about 1¼ cups)

1 celery stalk, diced (about ½ cup)

2 teaspoons minced fresh ginger root

5 cups Chicken or Vegetable Broth (pages 16, 20), or water

3 cups diced pumpkin (fresh or frozen)

1 small sweet potato, peeled and sliced (about 1 cup)

¼ cinnamon stick

¼ teaspoon freshly ground nutmeg, or to taste

½ cup dry white wine

½ cup evaporated skim or whole milk

2 teaspoons freshly squeezed lime juice

½ teaspoon salt, or to taste

½ cup heavy cream, chilled

Heat the butter in a soup pot over medium heat. Add the garlic, onion, celery, and half the ginger. Cook, stirring occasionally, until the onions and celery are softened, 8–10 minutes.

Add the broth, pumpkin, sweet potato, cinnamon stick, and nutmeg. Bring to a simmer and cook until the pumpkin is very tender, about 30 minutes.

Remove the cinnamon stick and discard. Puree the soup until quite smooth. Strain through a fine sieve for an exceptionally smooth texture, optional.

Return the soup to medium heat. Add the wine, milk, lime juice, and salt to taste. Stir to combine well and reheat just below a simmer.

Whip the chilled heavy cream to medium peaks and fold in the remaining ginger.

Serve the soup in heated bowls, garnished with a dollop of the ginger-flavored cream.

apple soup

This soup is a delicate blend of tart Granny Smith apple and sweet caramelized onion. Wait until just before serving to cut the red apple garnish so that it doesn't turn brown. Or, hold the apple slices in a small bowl of water with half a lemon squeezed into it. Pat the apple slices dry before garnishing the soup.

MAKES 8 SERVINGS

4 tablespoons unsalted butter or vegetable oil

4 onions, thinly sliced (about 5 cups)

4 Granny Smith apples, peeled, cored, and diced (about 4 cups)

1/4 cup all-purpose flour

1 quart Vegetable Broth (page 20) or water

3 cups apple cider or juice

Sachet: 3–4 parsley stems, 2 whole cloves, and 1 garlic clove enclosed in a teaball or tied in a cheesecloth pouch

1/2 cup heavy cream, heated

Salt, to taste

Freshly ground white pepper, to taste

8 thin slices Red Delicious apple

Melt the butter in a soup pot over medium heat. Add the onions and cook until golden brown, 5–8 minutes. Add the apples and continue to cook, 2 minutes.

Add the flour and stir well with a wooden spoon. Cook over medium heat, 1 minute. Add the broth in batches, using a whisk to work out any lumps between each addition. Add the apple cider and sachet. Bring the soup to a simmer and continue to simmer gently, 30 minutes. Stir the soup occasionally and skim as necessary.

Discard the sachet and strain the soup through a sieve, reserving the liquid. Puree the solids and return them to the soup pot. Add enough reserved liquid to achieve a soup consistency. Add the cream and blend well. Return to a simmer. Season with salt and white pepper. Serve in heated bowls, each garnished with a slice of red apple.

cream of chicken soup

The success of this velvety soup relies on a rich broth made by simmering a full-flavored stewing hen in chicken broth. The result is known as a double broth. If you already have a rich broth, use it to poach two chicken breasts. Cool and dice or shred the meat for the soup garnish, and begin the recipe by cooking the vegetables.

MAKES 8 TO 10 SERVINGS

1 stewing hen (about 3 pounds)

3 quarts Chicken Broth (page 16)

¼ cup unsalted butter (½ stick)

1 leek, white and light green parts, sliced thinly (about 1¼ cups)

1 onion, thinly sliced (about 1¼ cups)

½ celery stalk, thinly sliced (about ¼ cup)

2 tablespoons minced shallots

¼ cup all-purpose flour

Sachet: 4–5 black peppercorns, 1 bay leaf, 4–5 parsley stems, 1 garlic clove, and 1 sprig fresh or ½ teaspoon dried thyme enclosed in a large teaball or tied in a cheesecloth pouch

1 cup heavy cream, heated

Salt, to taste

Freshly ground white pepper, to taste

Place the hen and giblets (discard the liver or reserve for another use) in a tall soup pot. Cover with cold broth. Bring to a simmer, skimming as necessary. Simmer gently until the hen is fork-tender, about 1 hour, continuing to skim as needed.

Remove the hen from the broth and let cool. Dice or shred the breast meat for a garnish; reserve the remaining meat for another use. Strain the broth through a fine sieve and set aside.

Clean the soup pot and place over medium heat. Melt the butter, then add the leek, onion, celery, and shallots. Stir to coat evenly with butter. Cover the pot and cook the vegetables, stirring occasionally, until tender and translucent, 4–6 minutes.

Add the flour and cook over low heat, 6–7 minutes, stirring almost constantly. Gradually add 8 cups of the broth, using a whisk to work out any lumps after each addition (refrigerate or freeze any remaining broth for another use). Add the sachet and bring to a simmer. Simmer gently, 45 minutes, stirring occasionally and skimming as necessary.

Remove the sachet and discard. Strain the soup through a fine sieve, reserving the liquid. Puree the solids and return to the liquid. Strain the soup once more.

Return the soup to a simmer. Remove from the heat and add the hot cream. Add the diced or shredded breast meat. Season with salt and white pepper. Serve in heated bowls.

waterzooi (belgian cream of chicken soup)

Waterzooi is richer and slightly thicker than regular Cream of Chicken Soup due to the addition of a liaison, *a mixture of egg yolks and cream. Liaisons are added to hot liquid using a process known as* tempering. *This simply means that the temperature of the liaison must be raised gently to keep the yolks from instantly scrambling, as might happen if the liaison were added directly to simmering liquid.*

MAKES 8 SERVINGS

1 stewing hen (about 3 pounds), or 1 whole roasting chicken breast

3 quarts Chicken Broth (page 16)

5 tablespoons unsalted butter, divided

3 tablespoons all-purpose flour

Sachet: 4–5 peppercorns, 1 bay leaf, 4–5 parsley stems, 1 clove garlic, and 1 sprig fresh or $^1/_2$ teaspoon dried thyme enclosed in a large teaball or tied in a cheesecloth pouch

2 tablespoons minced shallots

2 leeks, white and light green parts, diced (about $2^1/_2$ cups)

1 carrot, diced (about $^1/_3$ cup)

1 celery stalk, diced (about $^1/_2$ cup)

1 small yellow turnip, diced (about $1^1/_2$ cups)

2 white or yellow potatoes, peeled and diced (about 2 cups)

$1^1/_2$ cups heavy cream or half-and-half

2 egg yolks

Salt, to taste

Freshly ground white pepper, to taste

$^1/_4$ cup minced parsley or chives, optional

Place the hen and giblets (discard or reserve the liver for another use) or chicken breast in a tall soup pot. Cover with the broth. Bring to a simmer, skimming as necessary. Simmer gently until the hen is fork-tender, about 1 hour, continuing to skim as needed.

Remove the hen from the broth and let cool. Dice or shred the breast meat for a garnish; reserve the remaining meat for another use. Strain the broth through a fine sieve and set aside.

Clean the soup pot and place it over low heat. Melt 3 tablespoons of the butter in the pot. Add the flour and stir well with a wooden spoon. Cook, 3–4 minutes, stirring almost constantly. Gradually add 8 cups of the broth, using a whisk to work out any lumps after each addition. Add the sachet and bring to a simmer. Simmer gently, 45 minutes, stirring occasionally and skimming the surface as necessary. Discard the sachet.

Meanwhile, heat the remaining butter in a pot over low heat. Add the shallots, leeks, carrot, celery, turnip, and potatoes. Stir to coat. Add $^1/_2$ cup of the remaining broth (refrigerate or freeze any broth left over for another use). Cover the pot and cook the vegetables until tender, about 10 minutes. Remove from the heat.

Make a liaison by blending the egg yolks with the cream in a bowl. Temper by stirring in about 1 cup of the hot soup, then stir the tempered liaison mixture into the soup.

Add the breast meat and cooked vegetables to the soup. Season with salt and white pepper. Serve in heated bowls, sprinkled with parsley or chives, if using.

pureed soups

P UREED SOUPS ARE SLIGHTLY THICKER than cream soups and have a coarser texture. They are often based on dried peas, lentils, or beans, or on starchy vegetables such as potatoes, carrots, and squash. The entire soup is typically pureed, though occasionally, some of the solids are left whole for textural interest, as in the Senate Bean Soup (page 114). Pureed soups are frequently garnished with croutons or small dice of a complementary meat or vegetable.

MAIN INGREDIENTS FOR PUREED SOUPS

Broth or water are the most commonly used base liquids for pureed soups. Be sure to check the freshness of broths that have been stored before using them in a soup.

A great many pureed soups are based on dried beans, such as great Northerns, navy beans, lentils, black beans, and split peas. Some beans should be soaked for several hours before cooking, which allows the beans to absorb some liquid, shortening the overall cooking time for the soup, as well as allowing them to cook more evenly.

Other pureed soups are made from relatively starchy vegetables. These will normally require peeling and dicing or slicing. Since they are pureed before they are served, neatness is not critical. Relative uniformity of size is important, however, to allow all the ingredients to cook evenly.

Onions, garlic, carrots, celery, mushrooms, and tomatoes are all commonly found in pureed soups. Other vegetables are also suggested by specific recipes, such as sweet peppers. For extra flavor, these vegetables can be roasted or grilled beforehand.

SUPPORTING FLAVORS

Many pureed soups call for a bit of rendered salt pork, smoked ham, bacon, or other cured pork products. For some recipes, you might need to blanch these ingredients first to remove any excess salt by covering them with cool water, bringing the water to a simmer, then draining and rinsing. An alternative is to use a ham-based broth.

A variety of ingredients may be used to season pureed soups: chiles, dried mushrooms, diced meats, hot sauces, citrus zest or juices, and vinegars. Garnishes might include croutons, diced meats, chopped herbs, toasted or fried tortillas, salsas, and/or dollops of sour cream.

Though pureed soups are expected to be somewhat thick and coarse, they should still be liquid enough to pour easily from a ladle into a bowl. Their flavor should clearly reflect the major ingredient. The color will vary greatly according to the flavoring ingredients used.

One of the major complaints about pureed soups is that they are served when they are too thick. Remember, the consistency of any soup must be such that it can be eaten easily from a spoon. The spoon should not be able to stand upright in the soup. Observing the proper relationship between the flavoring ingredient and the liquid should assure that the soup has a pleasing, robust flavor, without becoming watery or too starchy during cooking and reheating. If necessary, the soup can be thinned with additional broth. Some of the other problems you may encounter when making pureed soups are discussed here.

- *Scorched taste.* Because most pureed soups are fairly starchy, they should be stirred frequently during cooking to prevent scorching. Using a heavy-gauge pot and moderate heat will also help to prevent scorching.

- *Separation of liquids and solids.* Some liquid may separate and rise to the top during storage. Fully reheating and stirring the soup well before serving will remedy this problem.

basic pureed soup method

 Cook the aromatic vegetables in fat.

Occasionally a recipe will call for minced bacon or salt pork, which should first be cooked over moderate heat until the fat renders. Then, add the onions, garlic, shallots, leeks, or other aromatic vegetables called for by the recipe. Cook them over moderately low heat, until a rich aroma develops (fig. 1). It is often appropriate to allow aromatics for a puree soup to cook long enough to take on a rich golden hue. Remember, this should be done over moderate heat to avoid developing a harsh flavor. For some soups, it can take as much as 20 to 30 minutes to properly cook these aromatics.

 Add the liquid and any long-cooking ingredients; bring to a simmer.

Beans, potatoes, squash, and other similar ingredients should be added at the same time that the liquid base is added to the soup pot (fig. 2). Keep in mind that the relative dryness of the ingredients makes it impossible to predict how much liquid might be needed to keep the soup at the correct consistency. If your beans are from a late harvest or have been stored for a long time, they will require up to one-third more liquid than younger, moister beans, to cook properly. If the soup looks thick as it simmers, it may need additional broth or water.

3.

> *Add additional ingredients at the appropriate time and simmer until all ingredients are very tender.*

Pureed soups, like all others, should be skimmed throughout cooking. The starchy ingredients in these soups can easily scorch on the bottom of the pot, so stir frequently, and monitor the cooking speed and temperature carefully. Add a sachet approximately 1 hour before the end of the cooking time and remove once the soup has extracted the right amount of flavor. The soup has simmered long enough when the ingredients mash easily (fig. 3).

4.

> *Puree the soup and adjust the consistency and seasoning.*

There are several choices when it comes to pureeing equipment (see page 3). Whichever you choose, allow soups to cool slightly before pureeing. If you use a blender or food processor (fig. 4), be sure the lid is completely closed. Otherwise, the soup could literally explode out of the machine when you turn it on, spraying you and your kitchen with hot food.

To control the texture and consistency of the finished soup, strain out the solids, puree them until smooth, then gradually reincorporate the liquid portion of the soup. (If you use a blender or food processor, you will need to add a little of the liquid, so that the machine can puree the solids easily.) It may not be necessary to incorporate all of this liquid, or it may be necessary to add a little more broth or water. At this point, the soup is ready to be seasoned, garnished, and served, or it may be cooled and stored according to the procedures outlined in chapter 1.

senate bean soup

According to legend, this soup was frequently found on the menu at the U.S. Senate dining room. When the weather became hot, it was discontinued. There was such an outcry, however, that it soon reappeared. Just to be certain that they would never be without their favorite soup again, the Senate actually passed a bill requiring that it be offered every day that the dining hall was open.

MAKES 8 SERVINGS

1¼ cups dry navy beans

2 tablespoons olive oil

2 carrots, finely diced (about ¾ cup)

2 celery stalks, finely diced (about 1 cup)

1 garlic clove, finely minced (about ½ teaspoon)

½ medium onion, finely diced (about ¾ cup)

1 quart Chicken or Vegetable Broth (pages 16, 20)

1 smoked ham hock

1 yellow or white potato, peeled and diced

Sachet: 3–4 whole black peppercorns and 1 whole clove enclosed in a large teaball or tied in a cheesecloth pouch

Salt, to taste

Freshly ground white pepper, to taste

Tabasco sauce, to taste

1 cup Garlic Croutons (page 183)

Sort through the beans, discarding any stones or bad beans. Place the beans in a large pot and pour in enough water to cover by at least 3 inches. Bring to a boil, then remove from the heat. Cover and soak for 1 hour. Drain the beans, rinse in cold water, and set aside.

Heat the oil in a soup pot over moderate heat. Add the carrots, celery, garlic, and onion. Cook over low to medium heat until the garlic has a sweet aroma and the onions are a light golden brown, about 5 minutes.

Add the beans, broth, and ham hock. If necessary, add enough water to cover the beans by about 1 inch. Bring to a simmer, cover, and cook, 1 hour.

Add the potato and the sachet. Continue to simmer over low heat until the beans and potatoes are tender enough to mash easily, about 30 minutes.

Remove the ham hock from the soup. When it is cool enough to handle easily, pull the lean meat away from the bone and dice. Reserve the meat.

Puree about half of the soup, until smooth. Return to the pot. If necessary, thin the soup with additional broth. Season with the salt, pepper, and Tabasco sauce.

Serve in heated bowls or cups, garnished with the diced ham and croutons.

FACING PAGE: Quick-soaking the beans (top left); simmering the beans with vegetables and a ham hock (top right); adding potatoes for the last 30 minutes (bottom left); trimming and dicing the ham garnish (bottom right)

puree of white bean soup

This rustic white bean soup has a sweet and gentle flavor, less exotic than that of the Puree of Black Bean Soup (page 117). If you'd like more texture in the soup, puree only half the beans, as is done in the Senate Bean Soup (page 114).

MAKES 8 SERVINGS

1 pound dry white beans

$^1/_3$ cup plus $^1/_4$ cup olive oil

2 leeks, white and light green parts, diced finely (about 2$^1/_2$ cups)

1 medium onion, diced finely (about 1$^1/_4$ cups)

1 carrot, diced finely (about $^1/_3$ cup)

1 celery stalk, diced finely (about $^1/_2$ cup)

2 garlic cloves, minced (about 1 teaspoon)

2 quarts Chicken or Vegetable Broth (pages 16, 20)

Sachet: 1 sprig fresh or 1 teaspoon dried rosemary, 1 bay leaf, and 4–5 parsley stems enclosed in a large teaball or tied in a cheesecloth pouch

2 cloves garlic, peeled, left whole

Salt, to taste

Freshly ground white pepper, to taste

8 Italian bread slices, toasted

1 cup grated Parmesan cheese

1 tablespoon minced fresh thyme

Sort through the beans, discarding any stones or bad beans. Place the beans in a large pot and pour in enough water to cover by at least 3 inches. Bring to a boil, then remove from the heat. Cover and soak, 1 hour. Drain the beans, rinse in cold water, and set aside.

Heat $^1/_3$ cup of the olive oil in a soup pot over medium heat. Add the leeks, onion, carrot, celery, and minced garlic. Cover the pot and cook, stirring occasionally, until the vegetables are translucent and tender, about 10 minutes.

Add the beans, broth, and sachet. Bring to a simmer and cook, covered, until the beans are tender, 1–1$^1/_2$ hours. From time to time, stir down to the bottom of the pot with a wooden spoon, to prevent the beans from sticking.

Meanwhile, heat the remaining $^1/_4$ cup olive oil in a small saucepan over medium heat. Add the whole garlic cloves and sauté until deep brown, being careful not to burn the cloves. Discard the garlic cloves and set the oil aside to cool.

Remove the sachet and discard. Strain the solids, reserving the liquid. Puree the solids. Return the puree to the liquid and bring the soup back to a simmer. If the soup is too thick, add additional broth.

Just before serving, season the soup with salt and pepper. Place a slice of toasted bread in the bottom of each heated soup bowl and top with half the grated Parmesan. Ladle the soup over the toast and sprinkle with the garlic oil and thyme. Pass the remaining grated Parmesan on the side.

puree of black bean soup

This delicious, hearty soup is simple to make, although soaking and simmering the beans takes some time. If you're in a hurry, you can substitute 7 cups of drained and rinsed canned black beans. Reduce the simmering time to thirty minutes. The flavor and texture will not be quite the same, but you will be sitting down to eat sooner.

MAKES 8 SERVINGS

1 pound dry black beans

⅓ cup extra-virgin olive oil

4 garlic cloves, minced (about 2 teaspoons)

2 leeks, white and light green parts, finely diced (about 2½ cups)

1 medium onion, finely diced (about 1¼ cups)

2 quarts Chicken or Vegetable Broth (pages 16, 20)

Sachet: 1 teaspoon cumin seeds, 1-inch slice fresh ginger, 1 dry hot chili, and 4–5 parsley stems enclosed in a large teaball or tied in a cheesecloth pouch

1 lemon, zest grated, juiced

Salt, to taste

Freshly ground black pepper, to taste

1 cup sour cream or plain yogurt

½ cup diced fresh tomato

⅓ cup sliced scallion greens

Sort through the beans, discarding any stones or bad beans. Place the beans in a large pot and pour in enough water to cover by at least 3 inches. Bring to a boil, then remove from the heat. Cover and soak, 1 hour. Drain the beans, rinse in cold water, and set aside.

Heat the olive oil in a soup pot over medium heat. Add the garlic, leeks, and onions. Cover the pot and cook, stirring occasionally, until the vegetables are translucent, about 10 minutes.

Add the beans, broth, and sachet. Bring to a simmer and cook, covered, until the beans are tender, 1–1½ hours. From time to time, stir down to the bottom of the pot with a wooden spoon, scraping the bottom of the pot, to prevent the beans from sticking.

Remove the sachet and discard. Strain the solids, reserving the liquid. Puree the solids, adding some of the reserved liquid as necessary to help the beans move. Return the pureed solids to the pot and bring back to a simmer. If the soup is too thick, add additional broth and stir well.

Just before serving, stir in the lemon juice and grated lemon zest, and season with salt and pepper. Serve in heated bowls, garnished with sour cream, tomato, and scallion.

puree of split pea soup

The bacon and ham hock add a traditional smoky flavor to this thick and heart-warming puree of vegetable and split peas. However, if you prefer a meatless version, omit the bacon and ham hock, substitute vegetable broth for the chicken broth, and replace the bacon fat with vegetable oil.

MAKES 8 SERVINGS

4 strips bacon, minced

1 medium onion, diced (about 1¼ cups)

1 carrot, diced (about ⅓ cup)

1 celery stalk, diced (about ½ cup)

1 leek, white and light green part, diced (about 1¼ cups)

6 cups Chicken Broth (page 16)

2 yellow or white potatoes, peeled and diced (about 2 cups)

½ pound split green or yellow peas, or lentils

1 smoked ham hock

Sachet: 1 bay leaf, 1 whole clove, 1 garlic clove, and 4–5 peppercorns enclosed in a large teaball or tied in a cheesecloth pouch

Salt, to taste

Freshly ground black pepper, to taste

1 cup Croutons (page 183)

Cook the bacon in a soup pot over medium-high heat until crisp and brown. Remove the bacon with a slotted spoon; drain on paper towels and set aside. Pour off all but 3 tablespoons of the bacon fat. Add the onion, carrot, celery, and leek; stir to evenly coat with fat. Cover the pot and cook the vegetables over medium-low heat, stirring occasionally, until the onion is tender and translucent, 6–8 minutes.

Add the broth, potatoes, peas, and ham hock. Bring to a simmer and cook over medium heat, 20 minutes, stirring occasionally. Add the sachet and simmer until the split peas are soft, about 30 minutes. Skim away any scum during simmering.

Remove the sachet and discard. Remove the ham hock and set aside to cool. When cool enough to handle, cut the ham off the bone, dice, and set aside.

Strain the soup through a sieve, reserving the liquid. Puree the solids and return them to the pot. Add enough of the reserved liquid to achieve a thick consistency. Blend well. Stir in the ham and bacon. Season with salt and pepper. Serve in heated bowls, garnished with croutons.

potage solferino (puree of vegetable and potato)

A small dice of parboiled vegetables brings fresh color and texture to this humble puree. For a garnish, try the Fried Shallots on page 203. Or, you might also use a slotted spoon to remove the crisp bacon bits in step 1, drain them on paper towels, and sprinkle them over the soup just before serving.

MAKES 4 TO 6 SERVINGS

2 tablespoons unsalted butter

4 slices bacon, diced

1 carrot, sliced (about ⅓ cup),
plus ¼ cup finely diced

1 stalk celery, diced (about ½ cup)

1 leek, white and green parts,
sliced (about 1¼ cups)

1 medium onion, diced (about 1¼ cups)

1 small yellow turnip,
peeled and diced (about 1½ cups)

¼ head cabbage, shredded (about 2 cups)

1 quart Chicken or Vegetable Broth (pages 16, 20)

2 yellow or white potatoes,
peeled and diced (about 2 cups)

Sachet: 1 bay leaf, 1 teaspoon chopped fresh or
½ teaspoon dried oregano, 4–5 black peppercorns,
1 garlic clove, and 1 teaspoon chopped fresh
marjoram or ½ teaspoon dried leaves enclosed
in a large teaball or tied in a cheesecloth pouch

¼ cup sliced green beans

1 small tomato, peeled, seeded, and chopped

1 tablespoon chopped parsley

Salt, to taste

Freshly ground black pepper, to taste

Melt the butter in soup pot over medium heat. Add the bacon and cook until the bacon is crisp and brown, 6–7 minutes.

Add the carrot, celery, leek, onion, turnip, and cabbage; stir to coat evenly. Cover and cook until the onion is tender and translucent, 4–5 minutes.

Add the broth, potatoes, and sachet. Bring to a simmer and cook until the vegetables are tender, 25–30 minutes.

Meanwhile, boil or steam separately the diced carrots and sliced green beans until just tender. Set aside to cool.

Remove the sachet and discard. Strain soup through a sieve, reserving liquid. Puree solids and return to the pot. Add enough of the reserved liquid to achieve a thick soup consistency.

Add the diced carrot, green beans, tomato, and parsley. Season with salt and pepper. Simmer until heated through, about 5 minutes. Serve in heated bowls.

puree of two artichokes

Artichoke lovers will adore this soup. It combines the flavors of Jerusalem and regular globe artichokes. Although the Jerusalem artichoke is not truly an artichoke (it's actually the tuber of a type of sunflower), it has a taste and texture not unlike that of an artichoke heart. It is believed that the name Jerusalem artichoke is derived from the Italian word for sunflower: girasole. Jerusalem artichokes, also known as sunchokes, are usually available from October to March. Choose those that are firm, not soft and wrinkled. Store in a plastic bag in the refrigerator for up to one week.

MAKES 8 SERVINGS

1 large globe artichoke (about 12 ounces)

2 quarts Chicken or Vegetable Broth (pages 16, 20)

1 cup Jerusalem artichokes

$^1/_2$ lemon

3 tablespoons unsalted butter

$^1/_2$ medium onion, diced (about $^3/_4$ cup)

1 celery stalk, diced (about $^1/_2$ cup)

3 tablespoons all-purpose flour

$^1/_2$ cup heavy cream

1 tablespoon fresh lemon juice, or to taste

Salt, to taste

Freshly ground white pepper, to taste

$^1/_4$ cup thinly sliced chives

2 tablespoons thinly sliced scallion greens

Cut off all but about 2 inches of the globe artichoke stem. Use a paring knife to trim away the tough outer part of the remaining stem. Place the artichoke and broth in a large non-aluminum saucepan and bring to a simmer. Cover and cook until the outer leaves are tender and pull away easily, about 35 minutes. (If necessary, weight the artichoke with a small inverted crock or heavy plate to keep it submerged while simmering.) When tender, remove from the broth and set aside to cool. Reserve the broth.

Meanwhile, fill a glass or stainless steel bowl with cold water and squeeze the $^1/_2$ lemon into it. Drop the rind into the water as well. Peel the Jerusalem artichokes with a stainless steel paring knife, placing each one in the lemon water as soon as it is peeled.

Melt the butter in a soup pot over medium heat. Add the onion and celery and cook, stirring occasionally, until the vegetables are translucent, about 5 minutes. Stir in the flour and continue to cook, 2 minutes.

Whisk in the reserved broth. Drain the Jerusalem artichokes, slice thin, and add to the broth. Bring to a simmer and cook, partially covered, 30 minutes (if the level of liquid drops, add more broth or water to keep it constant).

While the soup is simmering, scrape the flesh off the base of each artichoke leaf with the end of a teaspoon and reserve the flesh (the innermost leaves are very thin and will not yield any flesh; discard these). Use the spoon to scoop the hairy choke from the heart. Dice the heart and reserve for garnish.

Add flesh from the artichoke leaves and the cream to the soup. Puree. Return puree to cleaned soup pot and bring to a simmer.

Season soup with lemon juice, salt, and white pepper. Serve soup in heated bowls, garnished with diced artichoke heart, chives, and scallions.

roasted eggplant and garlic soup

Tahini is a paste made from sesame seeds. It can be found in most large supermarkets (often next to the peanut butter), as well as in shops that specialize in Middle Eastern and Asian foods. Roasting the garlic and eggplant in advance adds wonderful flavor and aroma to this hearty soup. Be sure to allow the vegetables enough time to take on a deep, rich hue.

To make this a substantial main-course soup, add drained, cooked chick peas, diced roasted peppers, cooked broccoli, and/or cooked cauliflower florets. Serve accompanied by warmed whole wheat pita bread. Garnish the soup with a drizzle of extra-virgin olive oil, chopped fresh parsley, and toasted pine nuts to add a final dash of flavor and texture.

MAKES 8 SERVINGS

4 garlic cloves, unpeeled	Preheat the oven to 350°F. Wrap the garlic cloves in a square of aluminum foil.
2 cups peeled, cubed eggplant	
1 yellow onion, diced (about 1¼ cups)	Combine the eggplant, onion, celery, and carrot in a baking dish large enough to hold them in a single layer.
1 celery stalk, diced (about ½ cup)	
1 carrot, diced (about ⅓ cup)	Place the garlic directly on the oven rack. Drizzle the olive oil over the vegetables. Cover the pan and roast, 20 minutes. Uncover, increase the heat to 400°F, and roast until the eggplant and garlic are very soft, about 15 minutes. When cool enough to handle, squeeze the garlic from its skin.
3 tablespoons olive oil	
1 yellow or white potato, peeled and diced (about 1 cup)	
1 quart Chicken Broth (page 16)	Combine the roasted vegetables with the potato, broth, and thyme in a soup pot and simmer until the potatoes are tender enough to mash easily, about 25 minutes. Remove the thyme and discard.
1 sprig fresh or ¼ teaspoon dried thyme	
2 tablespoons tahini	Add the tahini, salt, pepper, and lemon juice to the soup and whisk to combine the ingredients well. Simmer the soup, 2–3 minutes.
½ teaspoon salt, or to taste	
¼ teaspoon fresh ground black pepper, or to taste	Puree the soup. Return it to medium heat and simmer, 5 minutes, or until reduced to the desired consistency. Season with the salt, pepper, and/or lemon juice. Serve in heated bowls.
Freshly squeezed lemon juice, to taste	

puree of cauliflower soup

Choose a cauliflower with compact, creamy, white florets and green, crisp-looking leaves. Cauliflower can be stored in the refrigerator, wrapped tightly, for three to five days. Should parts of the cauliflower begin to discolor due to prolonged storage, simply cut these parts away and discard before making the soup.

MAKES 8 SERVINGS

2 tablespoons olive oil

1 leek, white and light green parts, chopped (about 1 1/4 cups)

1/2 medium onion, chopped (about 3/4 cup)

1/2 celery stalk, chopped (about 1/4 cup)

1 quart Chicken Broth (page 16)

1 head cauliflower, coarsely chopped (about 1 1/2 pounds)

1 small yellow or white potato, peeled and chopped (about 3/4 cup)

Sachet: 5 black peppercorns, 4 parsley stems, 1 sprig of fresh or 1/2 teaspoon dried thyme, and 1 bay leaf enclosed in a large teaball or tied in a cheesecloth pouch

1 cup milk, hot

1/2 teaspoon salt, or to taste

1/4 teaspoon freshly ground white pepper, or to taste

1/4 cup chopped chives, optional

Heat the oil in a soup pot over medium heat. Add the leek, onion, and celery. Cook, stirring occasionally, until the onions is translucent, 4–6 minutes.

Add the broth, cauliflower, potato, and sachet. Bring to a simmer and cook, stirring occasionally, until all the ingredients are very tender, about 35 minutes.

Strain the soup through a sieve, reserving the liquid. Puree the solids and return them to the pot. Add the milk and enough of the reserved liquid to reach a soup consistency. Blend well.

Season with salt and pepper. Serve in heated bowls, garnished with chives, if using.

potato, escarole, and country ham soup

Country hams have an altogether different taste and texture from that of boiled hams. They have been cured for lengthy periods and have a unique salty, smoky taste. Different parts of the country swear by their special curing techniques, as well as the way in which their pigs are fed, as the key to producing the ultimate ham. Ask your deli manager or butcher to help you find country ham or a suitable substitute.

MAKES 8 SERVINGS

1 tablespoon unsalted butter

1 onion, diced (about 1 1/4 cups)

1 leek, white and light green parts, minced (about 1 1/4 cups)

1 celery stalk, diced (about 1/2 cup)

1 garlic clove, minced (about 1/2 teaspoon)

1 quart Chicken Broth (page 16)

2 yellow or white potatoes, peeled and diced (about 2 cups)

1 sprig fresh or 1/2 teaspoon dried thyme

2 cups chopped escarole (about 8 ounces)

1 cup diced country ham

1/4 teaspoon salt, or to taste

1/4 teaspoon freshly ground black pepper, or to taste

Heat the butter in a soup pot over low heat. Add the onion, leek, celery, and garlic; stir until they are evenly coated. Cover the pot and cook until the vegetables are tender and translucent, 6–8 minutes.

Add the broth, potatoes, and thyme. Simmer the soup until the potatoes are tender enough to mash easily, about 20 minutes.

Remove the thyme and discard. Puree the soup. Return the soup to the pot and bring to a simmer.

Add the escarole and diced ham and simmer, 12–15 minutes, or until all the ingredients are tender.

Season with salt and pepper. Serve the soup in heated bowls.

potato soup with mushrooms and marjoram

This soup capitalizes on the marvelous flavor pairing of mushrooms and marjoram. If your market offers exotic mushrooms, substitute them for the white mushrooms suggested below. Another way to deepen the flavor is to infuse your chicken broth by simmering it with some dried mushrooms, such as porcini or shiitake.

MAKES 6 SERVINGS

2 tablespoons olive oil

1 yellow or white potato, diced (about 1 cup)

1 medium onion, diced (about 1¼ cups)

3 cups fresh white mushrooms, sliced (about 8 ounces)

1 leek, white part only, sliced (about 1¼ cups)

1 tablespoon chopped fresh marjoram

1 tablespoon chopped fresh chervil, optional

1 quart Chicken Broth (page 16)

1 cup sour cream

2 tablespoons unsalted butter

Salt, to taste

Freshly ground white pepper, to taste

Pinch freshly grated nutmeg, or to taste

Heat the olive oil in a soup pot over medium heat. Add the potato and onion, and sauté until the onion is golden, 5–7 minutes. Add the mushrooms and leek and cook, 2–3 more minutes. Add half each of the chopped marjoram and chervil.

Add the broth and bring to a simmer. Cook until the potatoes are tender, about 15 minutes.

Strain the soup through a sieve, reserving the liquid. Puree the solids and return them to the pot. Add enough of the reserved liquid to achieve a soup consistency. Blend well and return to a simmer.

Stir in the sour cream and butter. Season with salt, pepper, and nutmeg.

Serve in heated bowls, sprinkled with the remaining marjoram and chervil.

butternut and acorn squash soup

This soup has a rich, creamy texture that belies its actual calorie count. Feel free to use only one type of squash or to replace the squash with pumpkin. For a richer soup, whip a little heavy cream to soft peaks, fold in an equal amount of sour cream, and add grated fresh ginger to taste. Place a dollop of this ginger-scented cream on each portion.

MAKES 8 SERVINGS

1 tablespoon unsalted butter

1 onion, diced (about 1¼ cups)

1 carrot, diced (about ⅓ cup)

1 celery stalk, diced (about ½ cup)

1 tablespoon minced fresh ginger root

1 clove garlic, minced (about ½ teaspoon)

3–4 cups Chicken Broth (page 16)

2 cups cubed butternut squash

1 cup cubed acorn squash

½ yellow or white potato, peeled and sliced (about ½ cup)

¼ teaspoon salt, or to taste

¼ teaspoon freshly ground white pepper, or to taste

1 teaspoon grated orange zest

Heat the butter in a soup pot over medium heat. Add the onion, carrot, celery, ginger, and garlic. Cook, stirring frequently, until the onion is tender and translucent, 5–6 minutes.

Add the broth, squashes, and potato. Bring the broth to a simmer and cook until the squashes are tender enough to mash easily with a fork, about 20 minutes.

Strain the soup through a sieve, reserving the liquid. Puree the solids and return them to the pot. Add enough of the reserved liquid to achieve a soup consistency. Blend well. Return to a simmer.

Season with the salt, pepper, and orange zest. Serve in heated bowls.

puree of carrot and orange soup

The affinity of carrots and oranges is highlighted in this fruity soup. The hint of ginger adds an appropriate sparkle. Though this recipe calls for the soup to be served hot, it also makes a delicious cold soup.

MAKES 8 SERVINGS

4 tablespoons unsalted butter

2 leeks, white and light green parts, diced (about 2 1/2 cups)

1 medium onion, diced (about 1 1/4 cups)

1 1/2 pounds carrots, peeled and diced (about 4 1/2 cups)

1 1/2 quarts Chicken or Vegetable Broth (pages 16, 20)

1/4 cup orange juice concentrate

1 orange, zest grated and juiced

Sachet: 4–5 parsley stems and a 1-inch slice of ginger root enclosed in a large teaball or tied in a cheesecloth pouch

Salt, to taste

Freshly ground black pepper, to taste

1/4 cup watercress leaves

8 orange sections, optional

Heat the butter in a soup pot over medium heat. Add the leeks and onion. Cover and reduce heat to low. Cook, stirring occasionally, until tender, 8–10 minutes.

Add the carrots, broth, juice concentrate, and sachet. Bring to a simmer and cook, stirring occasionally, until the vegetables are very tender, about 30 minutes.

Remove the sachet and discard. Puree the soup mixture. If some texture is desired, do not puree completely. Return to the pot, warm thoroughly, and season with salt and pepper.

Serve in heated bowls, garnished with watercress leaves and orange sections, if using.

corn and squash soup with roasted red pepper puree

This simple soup, based on a freshly made garlic-and-basil broth, is a wonderful way to take advantage of fresh summer produce. If you crave a taste of summer in the middle of winter, you can also make this soup with frozen corn.

MAKES 4 TO 6 SERVINGS

6 cups water

3 fresh basil sprigs

1 garlic head, halved horizontally

2 tablespoons unsalted butter

1 cup diced onion

2 cups diced yellow squash (about 1 large squash)

3 cups fresh corn kernels (about 4 medium ears fresh corn)

Salt, to taste

Freshly ground black pepper, to taste

½ cup Roasted Red Pepper Puree (page 202)

Combine the water, basil, and garlic in a large saucepan. Bring to a simmer and cook, partially covered, 30 minutes, skimming if necessary. Strain the broth and reserve.

Heat the butter in a soup pot over medium heat. Add the onion and cook, stirring frequently, until translucent, about 5 minutes.

Add the squash and cook, stirring, 5 minutes.

Add the corn and broth and bring to a simmer. Season with the salt and pepper.

Puree the soup and strain it through a fine sieve.

Return the soup to a simmer. Adjust the seasoning with more salt or pepper, if necessary. Serve in heated soup bowls. Swirl some of the red pepper puree through each portion.

black bean and butternut squash soups

This two-in-one soup is beautiful to behold and tastes as good as it looks. It's impressive, yet ridiculously easy to prepare. If you'd rather use freshly cooked black beans, start with 1½ cups of dried beans. You can use the bean cooking liquid instead of water to prepare the bean soup.

MAKES 8 SERVINGS

FOR THE BUTTERNUT SQUASH SOUP:

½ tablespoon butter

1 onion, diced (about 1¼ cups)

1 carrot, diced (about ⅓ cup)

1 small butternut squash, diced (about 3 cups)

¼ cup honey

¼ teaspoon ground cinnamon

⅛ teaspoon ground allspice

Salt, to taste

FOR THE BLACK BEAN SOUP:

1 dried chipotle chile, stemmed

3 cups drained canned black beans, well rinsed

1 cup water, plus more as needed

¼ teaspoon dried oregano, preferably Mexican

¼ teaspoon chopped dried epazote, optional

¼ teaspoon ground cumin

Salt, to taste

MAKE THE BUTTERNUT SQUASH SOUP:

Melt the butter in a large pot over medium-low heat. Add the onion and carrot. Cook until the onion is tender, 4–6 minutes.

Add the squash and enough water to cover by about 3 inches. Simmer, uncovered, until the squash and carrots are fork-tender, about 30 minutes.

Stir in the honey, cinnamon, and allspice and simmer, 2 minutes.

Remove from the heat and let cool, 10 minutes.

Puree the soup in a blender until smooth. (Thin the soup with a little water if necessary.)

Pour the soup back into the pot and bring it to a simmer over medium heat. Season with salt. Reduce the heat to low and keep the soup hot until ready to serve.

MAKE THE BLACK BEAN SOUP:

Grind the chipotle chile into a powder in a spice grinder. Puree the ground chipotle, beans, water, oregano, epazote, and cumin in a blender until smooth. Thin with a little additional water, if necessary.

Bring the soup to a simmer in a medium saucepan over medium heat. Season with salt. Reduce the heat to low and keep the soup hot until ready to serve.

TO SERVE THE SOUP:

Simultaneously ladle equal amounts of the two soups side by side into a heated soup bowl. Serve immediately.

bisques & chowders

B ISQUES ARE THICK, RICH SOUPS traditionally based on crustaceans, such as shrimp, lobster, or crayfish, and thickened with rice, rice flour, or bread. The shells are usually pureed along with the other ingredients, giving the bisque a consistency like that of a cream soup, but with a slightly grainier texture.

Modern renditions of bisques may be based on ingredients other than shellfish, and rely on a vegetable puree or roux as the thickener. As a result, the contemporary distinctions between pureed soups and bisques are not always clear. A vegetable-based bisque, for instance, is prepared in the same manner as a puree soup. If the main vegetable does not contain enough starch to act as a thickener, rice or a starchy vegetable may be used to provide additional thickness. After the vegetables are tender, the soup is pureed until a smooth texture is reached.

Chowders are thick, chunky soups made with a base of broth or milk, usually thickened with roux, and they almost invariably contain potatoes, onions, and salt pork or bacon. The original chowders were hearty fisherman's stews, made with the catch of the day. The word chowder is derived from *chaudière,* the French name of the cauldron traditionally used to make this type of soup. Chowders are included in this chapter because, like bisques, they were traditionally made with seafood. And, as with bisques, some contemporary chowders are based mainly on vegetables. The steps involved in making chowders, however, are more akin to those used to make hearty soups, so please refer to chapter 3 for more information on the basic method used to make them.

MAIN INGREDIENTS FOR BISQUES

Broths are at the base of most bisques. They should be checked before use if they have been stored. Bring a small amount to a boil, and taste for any sour or off odors. Rice, rice flour, wheat flour, or bread should be on hand to thicken the broth.

If you are making a seafood bisque, coarsely chop shellfish meat and shells. Shellfish should be scrubbed clean, and fish should be trimmed and cut into chunks.

For vegetable bisques, peel, trim, and cut the main vegetable, according to type.

SUPPORTING FLAVORS

The aromatic combination of onions, carrots, and celery is used to enhance the main flavoring ingredient in many bisques. Other ingredients frequently used to add flavor and color include tomato paste or puree, paprika, brandy, wine, and vinegar.

Cream is a common finishing ingredient for bisques. Diced cooked pieces of the main flavoring ingredient are traditionally used for a garnishing.

EVALUATING THE QUALITY OF BISQUES

A bisque should reflect the flavor of the main ingredient. If cream is added to round out and mellow the soup, it should not mask the main flavor. Bisques should be slightly coarse or grainy, with a consistency similar to that of heavy cream. A crustacean bisque should be a pale pink or red, a mollusk bisque should be ivory, and a vegetable bisque should be a paler shade of the color of the main vegetable.

Bisques, like cream and pureed soups, may develop problems during preparation and storage. Some of these are discussed here.

- *Consistency too thick.* Bisques may thicken during storage. If this happens, the soup can be thinned with additional broth, but not with cream. Too much cream will disguise the flavor.

- *Weak flavor.* If the flavor is weak, the ratio of major flavoring ingredient to liquid was wrong, or the soup was not simmered long enough.

- *Dominant rice flavor.* If the ratio of rice or rice flour to liquid was wrong, the soup may taste too strongly of rice. Use only enough rice to adequately thicken the soup.

- *Uneven texture.* Proper pureeing and straining are essential. The solids must be thoroughly pureed, and the soup strained again once the pureed solids and the liquid have been recombined.

1.

2.

3.

4.

basic bisque method

 Prepare the flavor base.

For a lobster, crab, or other bisque: Sear the shells in hot oil. The shells help develop the flavor of a good bisque, so it is important that they be cooked until they turn deep red or pink (fig. 1). Stir them frequently, to cook well on all sides. Add aromatic vegetables to the seared shells and allow them to sweat over moderate heat to avoid developing a harsh flavor. It can take from 20 to 30 minutes to properly cook these aromatics. Once they are cooked, two optional ingredients may be added: tomato paste or puree, and brandy. If you use one of the tomato products, it should be cooked until it takes on a deep rust color. This process, known as *pinçage*, cooks the tomato paste or puree down so that it will contribute a deep, rich flavor that is not excessively sweet (fig. 2). Otherwise, the tomato product could give the soup a raw flavor. If desired, brandy can then be added and cooked out. This step also continues the process of developing a complex, refined flavor base for the finished bisque. Flaming the brandy will quickly reduce it and burn off some of the raw alcohol, leaving behind the brandy's flavor essence.

For a clam, mussel, or other mollusk bisque: Steam the shellfish in fish broth until they open. Strain and reserve the broth for use as the main soup liquid. Remove the shellfish meat from the shells and chop about half the meat to be added to the bisque; reserve the remaining meat for garnishing. Cook the aromatic vegetables in oil or butter.

For a vegetable bisque: Cook the main vegetables and aromatics in oil or butter.

 Add liquid, thickener, and additional ingredients.

If you are using rice or bread as the thickener, add the broth to the pot and simply stir the rice or bread into the soup at the appropriate time (fig. 3). If a bisque requires a long cooking time, the recipe may instruct you to add the rice or bread after the soup has simmered for a while (fig. 4). If you are using a roux, stir the flour into the fat and cook out the roux, then whisk in the broth. The bisque can also be thickened with a *slurry*, a solution of wheat flour, rice flour, or cornstarch dissolved in broth or water.

5.

6.

7.

Wine and additional herbs or other aromatics are generally added at this point. Remember to taste the bisque as it simmers and to remove the sachet once the best flavor has been reached.

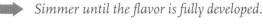 *Simmer until the flavor is fully developed.*

Bisques take about forty-five minutes to one hour to cook properly. At that point, all ingredients, except the shells, should be relatively tender, so that they will puree easily (fig. 5).

Bisques should be skimmed throughout the cooking time. Stir frequently and be sure to monitor the heat. Bisques, like any other soup with starchy ingredients, can scorch quickly if left untended for even a few minutes.

Taste the soup, so that you can modify it, if needed, during the cooking time. Add additional liquid, if necessary, to maintain the proper balance between liquids and solids.

Puree, strain, and finish the bisque.

A food mill is recommended for crustacean bisques (fig. 6). The entire contents of the soup pot, including crustacean shells, should be passed through the food mill. For other bisques, a blender or food processor can be used. To control the consistency of the finished bisque, you can strain and reserve the cooking liquid before pureeing the solids, then combine the puree with enough of the reserved liquid to reach a thick soup consistency. After pureeing and adjusting consistency, strain through a very fine sieve.

At this point, the bisque may be finished with ingredients such as cream, vinegar, additional seasonings, and garnishes, then served (fig. 7). Or, it may be cooled and stored according to the procedures outlined in chapter 1. If you plan to cool and store a bisque that is finished with cream, wait until just before serving to add the cream.

shrimp bisque

Much of the flavor in this soup comes from the shrimp shells. One-half to one pound of shrimp shells to are needed make this bisque, and it takes about four pounds of shrimp to yield a half-pound of shells. Don't buy shrimp just to get the shells. Instead, every time you shell shrimp for another use, save the shells in the freezer. When you have accumulated at least a half-pound of shells, then it's time to make bisque. For extra kick, you may add an additional quarter-cup brandy just before serving.

MAKES 8 SERVINGS

1/4 cup vegetable oil

1/2–1 pound shrimp shells

1 tablespoon minced shallots

1 leek, white part only, thinly sliced (about 1 cup)

1 celery stalk, thinly sliced (about 1/2 cup)

1 onion, thinly sliced (about 1 1/4 cups)

1/2 cup tomato puree

1 tablespoon sweet paprika

1/4 cup brandy

8 cups Fish Broth (page 19)

1/2 cup white wine

Sachet: 4–5 peppercorns, 1/2 bay leaf, 2–3 parsley stems, and 1 sprig fresh or 1/2 teaspoon dried thyme enclosed in a large teaball or tied in a cheesecloth pouch

1 cup long-grain white rice

1/2 cup heavy cream, heated

Salt, to taste

Cayenne pepper, to taste

1 cup diced, cooked shrimp

Heat the oil in a soup pot over high heat. Add the shrimp shells. Reduce the heat to medium and cook the shells for 10 minutes, stirring occasionally.

Add the shallots, leek, celery, and onion. Continue to cook until the vegetables soften, 4–6 minutes.

Add the tomato puree and paprika. Cook until the puree darkens, about 3 minutes.

Add the brandy and let the liquid boil away until nearly dry.

Add the broth, white wine, and sachet. Bring to a simmer and cook, 30 minutes.

Add the rice and simmer, 30 minutes, or until the rice is very soft.

Remove the sachet and discard. Puree the bisque (including the shells), preferably in a foodmill. Strain through a fine sieve.

Return to a simmer. Remove from the heat and add the heated cream. Blend well. Season with the salt and cayenne.

Heat the shrimp over low heat in a small amount of bisque. Divide the shrimp evenly among 8 heated bowls. Ladle the bisque over the shrimp and serve.

oyster bisque

This oyster bisque is quite easy to prepare and makes an elegant starter for a special meal, such as Thanksgiving or Christmas dinner. The bisque has good body and a flavor that is light and oystery, but not overly so.

MAKES 6 TO 8 SERVINGS

1½ quarts Fish Broth (page 19)

30 fresh oysters, scrubbed well

1 tablespoon unsalted butter

1 onion, diced (about 1¼ cups)

½ cup long grain white rice

1½ cups heavy cream, heated

¼ teaspoon salt, or to taste

Tabasco sauce, to taste

Worcestershire sauce, to taste

1 tablespoon chopped parsley

Bring the broth to a boil in a large pot. Add the oysters, cover, and steam until they open, about 12 minutes. Remove the oysters, discarding any that did not open. Strain the broth through a fine sieve, then through a coffee filter. Reserve the broth. Remove the oysters from the shells. Chop half the oysters. Set the whole and chopped oysters aside.

Heat the butter in a soup pot over medium heat. Add the onion and cook, stirring occasionally, until translucent, 4–6 minutes.

Add the oyster broth and rice. Bring to a simmer and cook until the rice is soft, about 20 minutes.

Puree the soup and place over low heat. Add the chopped oysters and the cream. Heat thoroughly, but do not simmer or boil.

Season with salt, Tabasco, and Worcestershire. Serve in heated bowls, garnished with the whole oysters and chopped parsley.

smoked tomato bisque

Smoked tomato adds an unusual twist to this bisque. There are two ways to smoke a tomato at home: indoors on the stove or outdoors on the grill. The directions for both methods follow the recipe. If you don't want to smoke a tomato using either method, the Roasted Tomato Bisque variation that follows is an excellent alternative.

MAKES 4 TO 6 SERVINGS

2 tablespoons vegetable or olive oil

1 onion, diced (about 1¼ cups)

1 celery stalk, diced (about ½ cup)

1 leek, white and light green parts, diced (about 1¼ cups)

2 cups Chicken or Vegetable Broth (pages 16, 20)

2 cups chopped plum tomatoes (canned or peeled and seeded fresh)

1 cup tomato puree

2 ounces chopped sun-dried tomatoes (about ½ cup)

1 tablespoon fresh thyme leaves, chopped

¼ cup long-grain white rice

3 tablespoons balsamic vinegar, or to taste

1 smoked plum tomato (see note), diced

Heat the oil in a soup pot over medium heat. Add the onion, celery, and leek. Cook, stirring occasionally, until translucent, 4–6 minutes.

Add the broth, plum tomatoes, tomato puree, sun-dried tomatoes, and thyme leaves. Bring to a simmer and cook, 30 minutes.

Add the rice and continue to simmer, 15 minutes. Puree the soup until very smooth. To give the soup an extremely fine texture, strain it through a fine sieve or cheesecloth-lined colander after pureeing, optional.

Return the soup to the pot. Stir in the vinegar and smoked tomato, and reheat to just below a simmer. Serve in heated bowls.

TO SMOKE TOMATOES INDOORS:

Scatter a thin layer of wood chips in the bottom of a disposable aluminum pan. Place a rack over the chips (use balls of aluminum foil to elevate the rack above the chips if necessary).

Cut the tomatoes in half lengthwise, remove seeds, and place cut-side down on the rack. Cover the pan tightly with another disposable pan or aluminum foil.

Place the smoker assembly over high heat until you can smell smoke.

Remove the pan from the heat, but keep covered, 3–4 minutes. Remove the skin from the tomatoes while still warm.

TO SMOKE TOMATOES OUTDOORS:

Prepare the grill. If using charcoal, stack the coals to one side. Scatter a thin layer of wood chips in the bottom of a disposable aluminum pan (or use aluminum foil to fashion a container for the chips).

Cut the tomatoes in half lengthwise and remove the seeds. Place the pan of chips on the rack above the hottest part of the grill. When the chips begin to smoke, place the tomato halves on the rack over the coolest part of the grill. Close the lid (make sure the air vent is open and positioned above the tomatoes if possible). Smoke, 5–7 minutes.

Remove the skin from the tomatoes while still warm. (If your grill has a built-in smoking compartment, follow manufacturer's directions).

ROASTED TOMATO BISQUE

Slice two ripe tomatoes about ½-inch thick, lay them on an oiled baking sheet, and roast in a 400°F oven, about 20 minutes. Use these roasted tomatoes to replace the sun-dried tomatoes in the preceding recipe, and omit the smoked tomatoes in the last step.

BELOW: Preparing the tomatoes for smoking (fig. 1); smoking the tomatoes over a burner (fig. 2); combining the ingredients and simmering (fig. 3); adding rice as a thickener (fig. 4); pureeing the soup (fig. 5); straining the soup through a sieve for a fine texture (fig. 6)

1.

2.

3.

4.

5.

6.

pumpkin bisque

Buy a variety of pumpkin meant for cooking when you make this bisque. Pumpkins meant just for carving are very fibrous and will not make a good soup. For added richness, garnish each portion of the bisque with a dollop of unsweetened whipped cream. For a playful presentation, serve the bisque in hollowed-out mini-pumpkins.

MAKES 6 TO 8 SERVINGS

2 tablespoons unsalted butter

2 garlic cloves, chopped (about 1 teaspoon)

1 celery stalk, diced (about 1/2 cup)

1 small onion, diced (about 1 cup)

1 leek, white part only, diced (about 1 cup)

1 pound pumpkin flesh, diced (about 3 1/2 cups)

2 quarts Chicken Broth (page 16)

2 tablespoons white wine

1/2 teaspoon grated ginger

Salt, to taste

1/2 teaspoon ground nutmeg, optional

Heat the butter in a soup pot over medium heat. Add the garlic, celery, onion, and leek. Cook, stirring occasionally, until the onion is translucent, 7–10 minutes.

Add the pumpkin and broth. Bring to a simmer and cook until the vegetables are tender, about 30 minutes.

Meanwhile, heat the wine in a small saucepan to a simmer. Immediately remove from the heat, add the ginger, and cover. Steep, 10 minutes, then strain the wine and discard the ginger.

Strain the solids from the soup, reserving the liquid. Puree the solids, adding enough of the reserved liquid to achieve a slightly thick consistency.

Add the wine to the soup and season with salt and nutmeg, if using. Serve in heated bowls.

new england seafood chowder

This thick, decadent chowder is packed with fish and shellfish. Round it out with a green salad, some crusty bread, and a bottle of dry white wine for an unforgettable meal.

MAKES 8 SERVINGS

8 chowder clams

1¼ pounds mussels, debearded (see page 48)

5 cups water

5 black peppercorns, crushed

2 fresh thyme stems,
plus 1 tablespoon fresh thyme leaves

2 parsley stems

½ bay leaf

2 tablespoons ground salt pork or
3 strips bacon, minced

1½ onions, diced (about 2 cups)

2 celery stalks, diced (about 1 cup)

½ cup all-purpose flour

2 large yellow or white potatoes, peeled and diced
(about 2 cups)

4 ounces cod fillet (about 1 small fillet)

4 ounces sea scallops, diced (about ⅔ cup)

1 cup heavy cream

1 cup milk

Salt, to taste

Freshly ground black pepper, to taste

Scrub the clams and mussels well in cold water. Place them in a large pot with the water, peppercorns, thyme stems, parsley stems, and bay leaf. Bring to a simmer, cover, and steam until the shells open, about 7 minutes. Discard any clams or mussels that do not open.

Remove the clams and mussels and strain the broth through a fine strainer, then through a coffee filter. Set the broth aside.

Remove the clams and mussels from their shells and dice. Set aside.

Heat a soup pot over medium heat and add the salt pork or bacon. Cook, stirring frequently, until the fat melts and the meat becomes crisp, 6–8 minutes.

Add the onions and celery. Cook, stirring occasionally, until tender, about 5 minutes.

Reduce the heat to low, add the flour, and cook, 3–4 minutes, stirring constantly with a wooden spoon. Stir in the thyme leaves, then add the reserved broth in batches, using a whisk to work out any lumps between each addition. Simmer, 30 minutes.

Add the potatoes and simmer until tender, about 20 minutes.

Add the cod fillet and simmer until cooked through, 4–6 minutes. Remove the cod, flake it apart, and return it to the chowder.

Add the clams, mussels, scallops, milk, and cream. Heat gently, but do not simmer, until the scallops are cooked, about 3 minutes.

Season with salt and pepper. Serve in heated bowls.

new england clam chowder

The Culinary Institute of America's version of the American classic—a silky, rich chowder based upon simple, wholesome ingredients. Chowder has a long tradition in New England, where family recipes are handed down from generation to generation.

MAKES 8 SERVINGS

3 dozen chowder clams

2½ cups bottled clam juice, or as needed

2 slices bacon, minced

1 medium onion, diced (about 1¼ cups)

2 tablespoons all-purpose flour

4 yellow or white potatoes, peeled and diced (about 4 cups)

3 cups heavy cream or half-and-half

6 tablespoons dry sherry, or to taste

Salt, to taste

Freshly ground black pepper, to taste

Tabasco sauce, to taste

Worcestershire sauce, to taste

Oyster crackers, as needed

Scrub the clams well under running water. Shuck, reserving the juices. Cut the larger clams in half. Mix the reserved juices with enough bottled clam juice to equal 3 cups.

Cook the bacon slowly in a soup pot over medium heat until lightly crisp, about 7 minutes.

Add the onion and cook, stirring occasionally, until the onion is translucent, 4–6 minutes. Add the flour and cook over low heat, stirring with a wooden spoon, 2–3 minutes. Whisk in the clam juice, bring to a simmer, and cook, 5 minutes, stirring occasionally. The liquid should be the consistency of heavy cream. If it is too thick, add more clam juice.

Add the potatoes and simmer until tender, about 20 minutes.

Meanwhile, place the clams and cream in a saucepan and simmer, until the clams are cooked, 5–8 minutes.

When the potatoes are tender, add the clams and cream to the soup base. Simmer, 5 minutes.

Stir in the sherry. Season with salt, pepper, Tabasco, and Worcesteshire. Serve in heated bowls, with oyster crackers on the side.

corn chowder with chiles and monterey jack

This chowder is best made with fresh corn on the cob, but if corn is out of season and you are desperate for corn chowder, you may substitute 3 cups frozen corn kernels that have been thawed. To avoid this altogether, make an extra batch or two at the height of corn season and freeze to enjoy later, in the dead of winter when fresh corn is but a distant memory.

MAKES 8 SERVINGS

6 ears corn, shucked

1 cup heavy cream

2 slices bacon, minced (about 1/4 cup)

1 medium onion, finely diced (about 1 1/4 cups)

1 red bell pepper, minced (about 1 cup)

1 celery stalk, finely diced (about 1/2 cup)

1 garlic clove, minced (about 1/2 teaspoon)

1 1/2 quarts Chicken Broth (page 16)

3 yellow or white potatoes, peeled and diced (about 3 cups)

3 medium tomatoes, peeled, seeded, and chopped, juices reserved (about 3 cups)

One 4-ounce can green chiles, drained and chopped

1 cup grated Monterey jack cheese

Salt, to taste

Freshly ground black pepper, to taste

Tabasco sauce, to taste

1 cup corn tortilla strips, toasted, optional

Cut the corn kernels from the cobs with a sharp knife, capturing as much juice as possible. Reserve 3/4 cup corn kernels. Puree the remaining corn, along with the heavy cream, in a food processor or blender. Set aside.

Cook the bacon in a soup pot over medium heat until crisp, about 8 minutes. Add the onion, pepper, celery, and garlic. Cover and reduce the heat to low. Cook, stirring occasionally, until the vegetables are tender, 10–12 minutes.

Add the broth, potatoes, and tomatoes, including their juices. Bring to a simmer and cook, covered, until the potatoes are tender, about 20 minutes. Skim any fat from the surface of the soup and discard.

Add the pureed corn and cream, reserved corn kernels, and chiles and cheese. Warm the soup. Season with salt, pepper, and Tabasco. Serve in heated bowls, garnished with tortilla strips, if using.

SMOKED CORN AND CHILE CHOWDER
WITH MONTEREY JACK

Do not try this smoking process unless you have a well-ventilated kitchen. Turn the exhaust fan on high and monitor constantly.

Substitute 2 fresh poblano chiles for the canned green chiles. Core and remove the seeds from the poblanos and red bell pepper. Cut into large flat pieces, approximately 4-inches square.

To smoke the corn and peppers, place fine wood chips in a disposable aluminum roasting pan fitted with a wire rack (if your rack does not have feet, use balls of aluminum foil to raise the rack a few inches above the wood chips). Use only wood chips that are specifically meant for smoking food. Have ready a fitted cover or aluminum foil large enough to cover the pan. Heat the roasting pan over high heat until the wood chips begin to smolder and smoke.

Place the corn and pepper sections on the wire rack over the smoking chips. If the chips are smoldering and creating sufficient smoke, remove the pan from the heat. Otherwise, reduce the heat to low. The idea is to keep the chips smoldering, but to keep them from catching fire. Cover tightly with the lid or aluminum foil and allow the vegetables to smoke for about 15–20 minutes. Remove the foil and allow the vegetables to cool. Dice the sections of red pepper and poblano chile.

Proceed with the master recipe, adding the poblanos along with the red pepper.

manhattan clam chowder

This is the classic mid-Atlantic clam chowder, not to be confused with New England's version. So disturbing is the inclusion of toma-toes to New Englanders that legislation was passed in Massachusetts making it illegal to add tomatoes to clam chowders. Fresh clams will, of course, make the best chowder, but, if you wish, you can substitute 3/4 cup canned clam meat and 3/4 cup bottled clam juice for the fresh clams and juices.

MAKES 8 SERVINGS

2 slices bacon, minced

3 dozen chowder clams, shucked, juices reserved

2 leeks, white and light green parts, diced (about 2¹/₂ cups)

1 medium onion, diced (about 1¹/₄ cups)

1 carrot, diced (about ¹/₃ cup)

1 celery stalk, diced (about ¹/₂ cup)

1 red bell pepper, seeds and ribs removed, diced (about 1 cup)

2 garlic cloves, minced (about 1 teaspoon)

2 canned plum tomatoes, seeded and coarsely chopped

2 yellow or white potatoes, peeled and diced (about 2 cups)

3 cups bottled clam juice

1 cup tomato juice

1 bay leaf

Pinch dried thyme

Salt, to taste

Freshly ground black pepper, to taste

Tabasco sauce, to taste

Cook the bacon in a soup pot over medium heat until crisp and browned, about 10 minutes.

Add the leeks, onion, carrot, celery, pepper, and garlic. Cover the pot and cook over medium-low heat, stirring occasionally, until the vegetables are soft and translucent, about 10 minutes.

Add the tomatoes, potatoes, clam broth, tomato juice, bay leaf, and thyme. Bring to a simmer and cook until the potatoes are tender, 15–20 minutes. Add the clams with their juices and simmer until the clams are cooked, 5–10 minutes more.

Using a shallow, flat spoon, remove any surface fat and discard. Remove the bay leaf and season to taste with salt, pepper, and Tabasco. Serve in heated bowls.

MANHATTAN FISH CHOWDER

Replace the clams with 1 pound of lean, boneless fish such as fresh cod, pollock or haddock, cut into 1-inch dice. Use fish broth (page 19) instead of the clam juice.

crab and mushroom chowder

Many supermarkets now carry a decent selection of more unusual mushroom varieties, such as shiitake, oyster, and cremini. You can make this delicious chowder using a single variety or a combination. Avoid white mushrooms, though; they don't have the flavor and texture needed for this hearty soup.

MAKES 8 SERVINGS

5 cups assorted mushrooms (about 1 pound)

6 tablespoons unsalted butter, divided

1/2 onion, diced (about 3/4 cup)

1/2 celery stalk, diced (about 1/2 cup)

1/2 leek, white and light green parts, diced (about 1/2 cup)

4 garlic cloves, minced (about 2 teaspoons)

1/2 cup all-purpose flour

1 quart Chicken Broth (page 16)

2 russet potatoes, peeled and diced (about 2 1/4 cups)

3/4 cup milk

3 teaspoons dry sherry

2 tablespoons heavy cream

1 teaspoon salt, or to taste

1 teaspoon freshly ground black pepper, or to taste

10 ounces lump backfin crabmeat, picked over for shells

Cut the stems from the mushrooms and slice the caps. Set the caps aside. Simmer the stems in 3/4 cup water, 30 minutes, to make a mushroom broth. Strain the broth and set aside.

Heat 5 tablespoons of the butter in a large soup pot. Add the onion, celery, leek, and garlic. Cook, stirring occasionally, until tender, 4–6 minutes.

Add the flour and cook, stirring, for 3–4 minutes. Gradually whisk in the chicken broth and bring to a simmer. Cook, 15 minutes. Strain through a sieve, pressing hard on the solids to recover as much thickened broth as possible. Return the broth to a simmer and discard the solids.

Add the potatoes to the broth and simmer until tender, about 15 minutes. Remove the pot from the heat and add the milk, sherry, and heavy cream. Season to taste with salt and pepper.

Meanwhile, melt the remaining tablespoon of butter in a skillet over medium heat. Add the sliced mushroom caps and sauté until tender, 7–10 minutes. Add the mushroom broth, stirring and scraping the bottom of the pan with a wooden spoon to loosen any particles of mushroom stuck to the pan. Season with salt and pepper.

Stir the mushrooms with their liquid and the crabmeat into the chowder. Check the seasoning. Serve in heated bowls.

oyster stew

This stew is a quick, elegant dish traditionally served on New Year's Eve in various parts of the country. If you don't want to shuck the oysters yourself, use one pint shucked oysters.

MAKES 8 SERVINGS

24 fresh oysters, shucked, juices reserved

4 bacon slices, minced

1 onion, minced (about 1¼ cups)

¼ cup all-purpose flour

1½ quarts milk

1 bay leaf

1 cup heavy cream, heated

½ teaspoon salt, or to taste

¼ teaspoon freshly ground black pepper, or to taste

Oyster crackers

Drain the oysters in a colander over a bowl. Reserve the juice.

Heat a soup pot over medium heat. Add the bacon and cook until crisp, 6–8 minutes. Transfer the bacon to a paper towel-lined plate.

Add the onion to the bacon fat and cook until translucent, about 6 minutes. Do not brown.

Reduce the heat to low, add the flour, and cook, 3–4 minutes, stirring constantly with a wooden spoon.

Add the milk and reserved oyster juice in batches, using a whisk to work out any lumps between each addition. Add the bay leaf and simmer, 20 minutes, skimming as necessary.

Add the whole oysters and continue to simmer until the oysters are barely cooked, about 5 minutes. Remove from heat.

Add the hot cream and season with salt and pepper. Serve in heated bowls, garnished with the reserved bacon and oyster crackers.

fennel and potato chowder

Fennel, which is sometimes labeled anise in supermarkets, is a vegetable with a broad, bulbous base that can be eaten raw or cooked. It has a delicate and very mild sweet licorice flavor. If you happen to find fennel with the feathery, dill-like tops still attached, chop some to use as a garnish. This is not a thickened chowder, so if you prefer a thicker consistency, try pureeing half the soup and mixing it with the unpureed half.

MAKES 8 SERVINGS

4 tablespoons unsalted butter

2 leeks, white and light green parts, diced (about 2½ cups)

1 onion, finely diced (about 1¼ cups)

1 shallot, minced (about 2 tablespoons)

1 fennel bulb, core removed, diced (about 1½ cups)

6 cups Chicken or Vegetable Broth (pages 16, 20)

4 yellow or white potatoes, peeled and diced (about 4 cups)

1 cup heavy cream or half-and-half, heated

Salt, to taste

Freshly ground white pepper, to taste

6 tablespoons minced chives or sliced scallions

Melt the butter in a soup pot over medium heat. Add the leeks, onion, shallot, and fennel. Stir to coat evenly. Cover and cook until the onion is tender and translucent, 4–5 minutes.

Add the broth and potatoes. Bring to a simmer and cook until the potatoes are tender, 20–25 minutes. Stir occasionally during simmering and skim as necessary.

Add the cream, blend well, and return to a simmer. Season to taste with salt and white pepper. Serve in heated bowls, garnished with chives or scallions.

CHAPTER SEVEN
cold soups

GAZPACHO ❖ FRESH SPRING PEA PUREE WITH MINT ❖ CHILLED CREAM OF AVOCADO SOUP ❖ COLD CARROT BISQUE ❖ CHILLED CARAWAY SQUASH BISQUE ❖ VICHYSSOISE ❖ CHILLED POTATO SOUP WITH TOMATO AND BASIL ❖ KH'YAAF B'LUBBAN ❖ COLD TOMATO AND ZUCCHINI SOUP ❖ BEET-FENNEL-GINGER SOUP ❖ CHILLED INFUSION OF FRESH VEGETABLES ❖ COLD CANTALOUPE CREAM SOUP ❖ CANTALOUPE SOUP WITH LIME GRANITÉ ❖ WHITE GRAPE GAZPACHO WITH TOASTED ALMONDS AND DILL ❖ COLD STRAWBERRY SOUP ❖ CHILLED RED PLUM SOUP

J ust as a steaming hot bowl of soup can warm you to the core on a freezing winter's day, so a cold soup holds the power to cool you on a blazing hot summer's day. Cold soups are usually served as appetizers or desserts, though they are refreshing whenever they are served.

Many of the soups found in the previous chapters will take very well to being served cold. Cold soups can be rich, as in the case of cream soups, or bold and robust, as in the case of pureed soups. Whenever you intend to serve any food chilled, be sure to taste it carefully at the correct serving temperature. Cold foods often require stronger seasoning than hot foods. Remember to allow soups sufficient time to develop their flavor. Some soups are at their best and ready to serve as soon as they are prepared. Other soups develop a more complex and satisfying flavor if they are allowed to mellow in the refrigerator for several hours or overnight.

COLD VEGETABLE AND FRUIT SOUPS

Cold vegetable and fruit soups are often popular hot-weather offerings around the world. Many cuisines have special cold soups featuring a seasonal vegetable or fruit.

Vegetable or fruit soups are usually made by pureeing or chopping vegetables and/or fruits fine enough to reach a soup-like consistency. These soups range in texture from the appealing coarseness of a gazpacho to the velvety smoothness of a chilled melon soup. Broth or juice is often added to the vegetables or fruits to loosen the puree enough to create a good consistency. Other ingredients, such as cream, milk, buttermilk, garnishes, or granités can be added to the soup for extra flavor, color, or texture.

COLD CREAMED SOUPS

Vichyssoise (page 165) is a classic example of a cold creamed soup. It is made by preparing a chilled purée of potato and leek that is enriched with half-and-half. Other cold creamed soups are made by preparing a cream or velouté soup, as illustrated in chapter 3. After chilling, they are typically finished by adding chilled cream, yogurt, or creme fraîche.

When you taste and evaluate your cold cream soup, pay attention to the texture and consistency. Cold cream soups should have the same velvety, smooth texture as hot cream soups. Cold soups may thicken as they cool, so be certain that you have adjusted the consistency to make a soup that is creamy but not stiff. Good cold creamed soups should not leave your mouth feeling coated with fat, so keep the amount of cream in proportion to the other ingredients.

COLD CLEAR SOUPS

Cold clear soups, like the Chilled Infusion of Fresh Vegetables on page 170, require a rich, full-bodied, clarified broth or juice. Infusions, essences, or well-strained purees are often used to the create the special character of these soups. Some clear soups are thickened with a little gelatin. Jellied clear soups should barely hold their shape, and should melt in the mouth instantly.

gazpacho

This tangy marriage of fresh tomato, cucumber, pepper, and onion is a summer favorite. The flavor of gazpacho improves if allowed to chill overnight, but thereafter this soup has a short shelf life, because the tomatoes sour very quickly. It is best prepared no more than a day or two before it will be eaten.

MAKES 8 SERVINGS

3 medium ripe tomatoes, peeled, seeded, and finely diced (about 3 cups); reserve juices

2 cucumbers, peeled, seeded and finely diced (about 2 cups)

1 medium onion, finely diced (about 1¼ cups)

1 medium red bell pepper, finely diced (about 1 cup)

2 garlic cloves, minced (about 1 teaspoon)

2 tablespoons tomato paste

2 tablespoons extra-virgin olive oil

2 tablespoons minced fresh herbs such as tarragon, thyme, and/or parsley

3 cups canned tomato juice

¼ cup red-wine vinegar, or to taste

Juice of ½ lemon, or to taste

¼ teaspoon salt, or to taste

¼ teaspoon cayenne pepper, or to taste

1 cup Croutons (page 183)

½ cup thinly sliced chives or scallion greens

Reserve 2 tablespoons each of the tomato, cucumber, onion, and pepper, for garnish.

Puree the remaining tomato, cucumber, onion, and pepper in a food processor or blender along with the garlic, tomato paste, olive oil, and herbs until fairly smooth, but with some texture remaining.

Transfer to a mixing bowl and stir in the tomato juice along with the red-wine vinegar, lemon juice, salt, and cayenne to taste. Cover and chill thoroughly, at least 3 hours, but preferably overnight.

After chilling, check the seasoning. Serve in chilled bowls, garnished with the reserved vegetables, croutons, and chives.

preparation tip

If the gazpacho is too thin for your taste, add about 1 cup of freshly made white bread crumbs before chilling. If it's too thick, add more tomato juice or water.

If the soup will be served before a seafood main course, try substituting fish broth or clam juice for part of the tomato juice.

fresh spring pea puree with mint

This delicate soup captures the essence of fresh peas. It's a great recipe to try if you have a bumper crop of peas, or if you're looking for an unusual soup to serve to company. Technically, you could make this soup with frozen peas, but it's not recommended; the flavor just won't be the same.

MAKES 8 SERVINGS

2 tablespoons olive oil

1¼ cups minced leeks, white and light green parts

1¼ cups minced onions

6 cups fresh peas

5 cups Vegetable Broth (page 20)

Sachet: 6 parsley stems and 3 white peppercorns enclosed in a large teaball or tied in a cheesecloth pouch

4 cups shredded green-leaf lettuce

¾ cup light cream or half-and-half, cold

½ teaspoon salt, or to taste

½ teaspoon freshly ground white pepper, or to taste

2 tablespoons finely shredded mint or chervil

Heat the olive oil in a soup pot over medium heat. Add the leeks and onions. Cover and cook, stirring occasionally, until the onions are soft and translucent, 4–6 minutes. Add the peas, cover, and cook, 2 minutes.

Add the vegetable broth and sachet. Bring to a simmer, cover, and cook until all the ingredients are very tender, about 45 minutes.

Add the lettuce and simmer until wilted, about 5 minutes.

Remove the sachet and discard. Puree the soup in a food processor or blender until smooth. Cover and chill thoroughly.

Just before serving, add the chilled cream to the soup. Season with salt and pepper. Stir in the mint or chervil and serve in chilled bowls.

chilled cream of avocado soup

This soup, one of the easiest in this book, manages to preserve the elusive flavor of the avocado. Use only very ripe avocados for this soup. If you buy avocados that aren't ripe, you can speed the ripening process by placing them in a closed paper bag with an apple. The apple will give off ethylene gas, which accelerates ripening.

You can garnish this soup with the suggested tomato and tortilla strips, or for a more elegant (albeit expensive) touch, try garnishing with lump crabmeat, cooked fresh corn kernels, and a touch of finely diced red pepper tossed with a dash of lemon or lime juice.

MAKES 4 TO 6 SERVINGS

2 large ripe avocados

4–5 cups Vegetable Broth (page 20) or water, divided

$\frac{1}{2}$ teaspoon chili powder

$\frac{1}{4}$ teaspoon ground coriander

Juice of 1 lime

1 cup plain yogurt or heavy cream

Salt, to taste

Freshly ground white pepper, to taste

2 ripe plum tomatoes, peeled, seeded, and diced, optional

2 corn tortillas, cut into strips, fried, optional

Cut each avocado in half from top to bottom, following the contour of the pit. Remove the pit and scoop out the flesh.

Puree the flesh in a food processor or blender with 4 cups of the broth, the chili powder, coriander, and lime juice until very smooth. If the soup is too thick, add more broth. Transfer to a bowl, cover, and chill thoroughly.

Just before serving, blend in the yogurt or heavy cream. Season with salt and white pepper. Serve in chilled bowls, garnished with the tomato and tortilla strips, if using.

cold carrot bisque

If you don't own a juicer, look for fresh carrot juice at your local health-food store or juice bar. Try garnishing this soup with a dollop of whipped cream and a sprinkling of sliced chives. Or, for a touch of sweetness, garnish with homemade Candied Orange Zest (page 198).

MAKES 8 SERVINGS

½ tablespoon unsalted butter

⅓ cup minced onion

3 tablespoons minced shallots

½ tablespoon minced fresh ginger, or to taste

1 garlic clove, minced

5½ cups thinly sliced carrots (about 1¾ pounds)

5 cups Vegetable Broth (page 20)

2 tablespoons white wine

½ teaspoon ground cardamom

2 cups orange juice

½ cup light cream, cold

1½–2 cups fresh carrot juice

2 teaspoons salt, or to taste

Melt the butter in a soup pot. Add the onion, shallots, ginger, and garlic and sauté until the onion is translucent, 4–6 minutes.

Add the carrots, broth, wine, cardamom, and orange juice. Bring to a simmer and cook until the carrots are tender, about 30 minutes.

Puree the soup in a food processor or blender until smooth. Cover and chill thoroughly.

Just before serving, stir in the cream. Thin the soup with carrot juice to a barely-thick consistency. Season with salt, and serve in chilled bowls, garnished as desired.

chilled caraway squash bisque

Aromatic caraway seeds complement the subtle flavor of yellow squash in this delicate and unusual soup. Small squash are the best choice for this soup because they have small seeds. If you can only find large squash, remove the big seeds. Regardless of the size, select squash that are firm, bright, and free of spots or blemishes.

MAKES 8 SERVINGS

4 tablespoons unsalted butter

1 onion, finely diced (about 1$\frac{1}{4}$ cups)

1 celery stalk, finely diced (about $\frac{1}{2}$ cup)

1 carrot, finely diced (about $\frac{1}{3}$ cup)

1 leek, white part only, finely diced (about 1 cup)

6 cups Vegetable Broth (page 20) or water

4 small yellow squash, diced (about 4 cups)

1 yellow or white potato, peeled and finely diced (about 1 cup)

Sachet: 1 teaspoon caraway seeds, 1 garlic clove, and 1 sprig fresh or $\frac{1}{2}$ teaspoon dried thyme enclosed in a large teaball or tied in a cheesecloth pouch

$\frac{3}{4}$ cup heavy cream

Salt, to taste

Freshly ground white pepper, to taste

1 teaspoon lightly toasted caraway seeds

Melt the butter in a soup pot over medium heat. Add the onion, celery, carrot, and leek. Stir to coat evenly. Cover and cook until the onion is tender and translucent, 6–8 minutes.

Add the broth, squash, potato, and sachet. Bring to a simmer and cook, stirring occasionally, until the potato is tender, about 25 minutes.

Remove the sachet and discard. Strain the soup through a sieve, reserving the liquid. Puree the solids and return them to the soup pot. Add enough of the reserved liquid to reach the desired soup consistency. Blend well and simmer, 2 minutes. Transfer to a bowl and chill thoroughly.

Add the heavy cream and blend well. Season, with salt and white pepper. Serve in chilled bowls, garnished with toasted caraway seeds.

vichyssoise

This is the Culinary Institute of America's rendition of the traditional classic, first prepared by French chef Louis Diat at New York City's Ritz Carlton Hotel in 1917. Diat's chilled potato-and-leek soup sprinkled with chives was inspired by a favorite hot soup made by his mother in France.

MAKES 8 SERVINGS

1¹/₂ tablespoons vegetable oil

3 leeks, white parts only, finely chopped (about 3 cups)

¹/₂ onion, minced (about ³/₄ cup)

5 cups Chicken or Vegetable Broth (pages 16, 20)

3 russet potatoes, peeled and diced (about 3 cups)

Sachet: 2 whole cloves, 2 parsley stems, 2 black peppercorns, and ¹/₂ bay leaf enclosed in a large teaball or tied in a cheesecloth pouch

1¹/₂ cups half-and-half, chilled

1 teaspoon salt, or to taste

Freshly ground white pepper, to taste

¹/₄ cup thinly sliced chives

Heat the oil in a soup pot over medium heat. Add the leeks and onion and cook until tender and translucent, 4–5 minutes.

Add the broth, potatoes, and sachet. Bring to a simmer and cook until the potatoes are starting to fall apart, about 25 minutes. Remove the sachet and discard.

Puree the soup. Chill thoroughly.

Just before serving, add the cold half-and-half to the soup and season with salt and white pepper. Serve in chilled bowls, garnished with chives.

chilled potato soup
with tomato and basil

This soup was inspired by vichyssoise, the classic cold leek-and-potato soup. Here, it is updated with a topping of fresh tomatoes and basil,

a favorite flavor pairing. It could easily be served hot instead of cold. Replace the basil with oregano, tarragon, or chives, if you wish.

When fresh tomatoes are out of season, substitute sautéed or deep-fried leeks or onions.

MAKES 4 TO 6 SERVINGS

1 bacon slice, chopped

1 yellow onion, chopped (about 1¼ cups)

2 russet potatoes, peeled and sliced (about 2¼ cups)

1 quart Chicken or Vegetable Broth (pages 16, 20)

1 bay leaf

½ cup half-and-half, chilled, optional

½ teaspoon salt, or to taste

¼ teaspoon freshly ground black pepper, or to taste

Tabasco sauce, to taste

1 plum tomato, finely diced

2 tablespoons shredded fresh basil

Cook the bacon in a soup pot over medium heat until the fat is rendered and the bacon bits are crisp, 6–8 minutes.

Add the onion and cook, stirring frequently, until onion is tender and translucent, 3–4 minutes.

Add the potatoes, broth, and bay leaf and simmer until the potatoes are tender enough to mash, about 20 minutes. Remove the bay leaf and discard.

Let the soup cool slightly and then puree it. Transfer the soup to a container, cool to room temperature, and refrigerate overnight.

If necessary, the consistency may be adjusted by adding additional broth. Add the half-and-half to the chilled soup, if using. Season with salt, pepper, and Tabasco.

Serve in chilled bowls, garnished with the chopped tomato and basil.

kh'yaaf b'lubban
(chilled cucumber and yogurt soup)

Fans of Indian food will find this Lebanese soup familiar, as it is quite similar in flavor to the Indian condiment kheera raita, *also made with yogurt, cucumber, and mint. As with kheera raita, the cooling quality of this soup makes it a wonderful complement or second course following spicy-hot foods.*

MAKES 6 TO 8 SERVINGS

2 garlic cloves, minced

3 tablespoons chopped fresh mint

1 quart plain yogurt

1 cup whole milk

4 medium cucumbers, peeled, seeded, and finely diced

Salt, to taste

Mix the garlic with the mint in a small bowl.

Beat the yogurt and milk together with a wire whisk, or with a hand blender on medium speed, until smooth. Fold in the mint-and-garlic mixture with a rubber spatula.

Combine the cucumbers with the yogurt mixture and lightly season with salt. Cover and chill for several hours or overnight.

After chilling, check the seasoning and adjust. Serve in chilled bowls.

cold tomato and zucchini soup

This fresh-tasting soup, much like gazpacho, is a great way to make use of a summer bounty of fresh vegetables and herbs. If time permits, make it a day ahead of serving to let the flavors blend. Don't store it more than two to three days, though, because tomatoes can sour quickly.

MAKES 8 SERVINGS

1¼ pounds plum tomatoes, peeled, seeded, and chopped coarsely (page 36, about 4 cups)

2 cups tomato juice

1 onion, coarsely chopped (about 1¼ cups)

1 red pepper, seeded, ribs removed, and coarsely chopped (about 1 cup)

½ cucumber, peeled, seeded, and coarsely chopped (about ¾ cup)

1 medium zucchini, coarsely chopped (about 1½ cups)

¼ cup chopped fresh cilantro

¼ cup chopped fresh basil

¼ cup chopped fresh parsley

1½ tablespoons drained, prepared horseradish

1 tablespoon red-wine vinegar

3 garlic cloves, chopped

Vegetable Broth (page 20) or water, as needed

Tabasco sauce to taste

Salt, to taste

Freshly ground black pepper, to taste

½ cup Seasoned Croutons (page 183)

Combine all the ingredients, except the broth, Tabasco, salt, pepper, and croutons, in a blender or food processor and process, in batches if necessary. Process in short pulses to a coarse puree.

Pour into a bowl. If it is too thick, thin it slightly with broth or water. Season with the Tabasco, salt, and pepper. Refrigerate at least 30 minutes before serving.

Serve in chilled bowls, garnished with croutons.

beet-fennel-ginger soup

This unusual soup has great color and a masterful balance of flavor between the sweet beets and fennel, vegetal cabbage, and spicy ginger. It can be served hot as well as cold. If you find a fennel bulb with the tops still attached, save some of the nicest-looking sprigs to use as a garnish.

MAKES 8 SERVINGS

4 fresh beets, peeled and chopped (about 2½ cups)

4 cups chopped savoy cabbage (about 8 ounces)

1 fennel bulb, core removed, chopped (about 2 cups)

3 tablespoons chopped fresh ginger root

1 garlic clove, chopped

1½ quarts Vegetable Broth (page 20)

½ teaspoon salt, or to taste

¼ teaspoon freshly ground black pepper, or to taste

⅓ cup plain nonfat yogurt

1½ tablespoons fennel sprigs, optional

Combine the beets, cabbage, fennel, ginger, garlic, and broth in a soup pot. Bring to a simmer, cover, and cook until the vegetables are tender, about 40 minutes.

Strain the soup, reserving the liquid. Puree the solids with a small amount of liquid in a blender until smooth. Combine the puree with enough of the remaining liquid to achieve the desired consistency. Season with salt and pepper.

Serve in chilled bowls, garnished with a dollop of yogurt and a fennel sprig.

chilled infusion of fresh vegetables

You can adjust the suggested vegetable garnish in this soup to suit your taste, using more or less of any particular vegetable. Or you can use different vegetables entirely. It's up to you. Fava beans, also known as broad beans, resemble large lima beans. Some supermarkets carry frozen fava beans, and in the spring you may be fortunate enough to find fresh favas. Fava beans have a tough outer skin that must be removed before cooking: Blanch the beans for about thirty seconds in boiling water, then cool slightly and slip the beans from the skins. If the skins do not come off easily, blanch again for another thirty seconds. If you cannot find fava beans, simply substitute fresh or frozen lima beans.

MAKES 8 SERVINGS

3¹/₂ cups sliced leeks, white and light green parts, (about 1 pound)

1 cup sliced celeriac

¹/₂ cup minced shallots

1¹/₄ cups minced parsley

2 tablespoons sliced chives

2 quarts water, or as needed, divided

1 teaspoon minced garlic

1 thyme sprig

¹/₂ bay leaf

1 tablespoon salt, plus more to taste

³/₄ teaspoon freshly ground black pepper, plus more to taste

3 cups quartered ripe tomatoes (about 1¹/₂ pounds)

¹/₄ cup sliced baby carrots

¹/₄ cup small green peas, fresh or frozen

¹/₄ cup fava or lima beans, fresh or frozen

¹/₄ cup asparagus tips

¹/₄ cup peeled, seeded, and diced tomato

8 fresh chervil or flat-leaf parsley leaves (optional)

Make the vegetable infusion: Combine the leeks, celeriac, shallots, parsley, chives, garlic, thyme, bay leaf, salt and pepper with 1¹/₂ quarts water in a soup pot. Cover and simmer gently, 1 hour. Add a little water to bring it back to its original level, return briefly to a boil, remove from the heat, and allow to cool. Strain through a fine-mesh sieve or cheesecloth. Cover and chill thoroughly.

Meanwhile, make a tomato broth: Combine the tomatoes with 1¹/₂ cups water. Simmer gently, 30 minutes, then strain through a fine sieve or cheesecloth. Cover and chill thoroughly.

Bring about 1 inch of water to a boil in a saucepan. Add the carrots, cover, and pan-steam until tender. Using a slotted spoon, transfer the carrots to a colander and rinse under cold water to stop the cooking. Drain well and transfer to a bowl. Repeat with the peas, fava or lima beans, and asparagus tips, cooking each vegetable separately until tender. Add the diced tomatoes to the cooked vegetables and toss to combine. Cover and chill thoroughly.

Mix the tomato broth with the vegetable infusion. Taste and adjust the seasoning. Serve in chilled bowls, garnished with the vegetables and the chervil leaves, if using.

cold cantaloupe cream soup

This is a surprisingly delicate and pleasant starter to any meal served on a hot summer day. Sparkling wine or seltzer may be added to the soup just before serving. For an unusual presentation, serve the soup in wine glasses. Dip the rims of the glasses into lightly whipped egg whites, then into granulated sugar, and chill.

MAKES 8 SERVINGS

1 medium cantaloupe, peeled, seeded, and cut into large chunks (about 6½ cups)

1 quart apricot nectar

Juice of ½ lemon

2 tablespoons honey

Sachet: ½ teaspoon ground ginger, 3 whole allspice berries, 1 whole clove, and one 2-inch cinnamon stick tied in a cheesecloth pouch

1 cup half-and-half, chilled

½ cup plain yogurt

8 mint leaves

Place the melon, apricot nectar, lemon juice, honey, and sachet in a soup pot. Bring to a simmer and cook, stirring frequently, until the melon is tender, 10–15 minutes.

Remove the sachet and discard. Strain the soup through a sieve, reserving the liquid. Puree the solids in a food processor or blender. Combine the puree with enough reserved liquid to achieve the desired consistency. Chill thoroughly.

Whisk the half-and-half into soup. Serve in chilled wine glasses or bowls, garnished with a dollop of yogurt and a mint leaf.

cantaloupe soup
with lime granité

This chilled melon soup is perfect to serve at an elegant brunch. Choose a cantaloupe that is fragrant and feels heavy for its size. The netting on the cantaloupe should be well raised, and the blossom end should yield slightly to gentle pressure.

MAKES 8 SERVINGS

1 small (1¹/₂-pound) cantaloupe, peeled, seeded, and cut into large chunks (about 4¹/₂ cups)

Juice of 2 oranges

¹/₄ cup cornstarch

Juice of 1¹/₂ lemons

3 cups sparkling water

2¹/₄ teaspoons orange zest

2¹/₄ teaspoons lemon zest

¹/₂ cup sugar, or to taste

1 recipe Lime Granité (page 198)

Puree the melon and orange juice in a blender.

Dissolve the cornstarch in the lemon juice. Bring the water, orange zest, and lemon zest to a boil in a large saucepan. While stirring, add the cornstarch solution and continue to stir until the liquid returns to a simmer and thickens. Remove from the heat.

Add the melon puree and sweeten to taste.

Serve in chilled bowls, garnished with small scoops of lime granité.

white grape gazpacho
with toasted almonds and dill

White grapes are a surprising ingredient in this refreshing soup. Cream cheese, an unusual soup ingredient, gives the soup body. English cucumbers, otherwise known as hothouse or seedless cucumbers, are less bitter than regular cucumbers and have very few seeds. Because they are not coated with food-grade wax like most regular cucumbers found in supermarkets, they can be used peel and all.

MAKES 10 TO 12 SERVINGS

2 pounds white seedless grapes, rinsed well
(about 6$\frac{1}{2}$ cups)

1 English cucumber, diced
(do not peel, about 3 cups)

4 scallions, green parts only, sliced (about $\frac{1}{3}$ cup)

2$\frac{1}{2}$ cups half-and-half

1$\frac{1}{4}$ cups plain yogurt

$\frac{1}{4}$ cup cream cheese (about 2 ounces)

2 tablespoons white-wine vinegar

2 tablespoons extra-virgin olive oil

$\frac{1}{2}$ cup plus 2 tablespoons chopped fresh dill

Salt, to taste

Freshly ground white pepper, to taste

$\frac{1}{4}$ cup sliced almonds, toasted

Peel and halve 18 grapes. Reserve for garnish.

Puree the remaining grapes with the cucumber, scallions, half-and-half, yogurt, cream cheese, vinegar, olive oil, and $\frac{1}{2}$ cup of the dill.

Season with salt and white pepper. Chill thoroughly.

Serve in chilled bowls, garnished with the remaining chopped dill, grape halves, and almonds.

cold strawberry soup

This rich and creamy soup tastes just like melted strawberry ice cream, but not quite as sweet. Be sure to make this soup when straw-berries are at their peak.

4 cups strawberries

¹/₃ cup sugar

¹/₄ cup white wine, light rum, or vodka

3 cups heavy cream

3 cups apple juice

1 teaspoon fresh lemon juice

¹/₂ cup honey

Reserve 1 large berry for garnish. Hull the remaining berries, and combine with the sugar and wine or liquor. Refrigerate for 2–24 hours.

Puree the berries with their liquid. Add the remaining ingredients, mix well, cover, and refrigerate, at least 2 hours.

Cut the reserved strawberry into paper-thin slices. Serve the soup in chilled bowls, garnished with strawberry slices.

chilled red plum soup

This sweet-and-spicy soup is a beautiful purple color that hints at the fullness of its fruit flavor. It makes the perfect beginning or end to a summer luncheon or outdoor dinner. Choose plums that are ripe, but not extremely soft. If red plums are unavailable, black plums will also do well in this soup.

MAKES 8 SERVINGS

2¹⁄₂ pounds red plums, pitted and chopped (about 6 cups)

1 quart apple juice

Sachet: 3–4 black peppercorns, 1 large slice fresh ginger, 1 whole allspice berry, and ¹⁄₂ cinnamon stick enclosed in a large teaball or tied in a cheesecloth pouch

¹⁄₂ cup honey

Fresh lemon juice, to taste

6 tablespoons sour cream

2 tablespoons slivered almonds, toasted

Combine the plums, apple juice, sachet, and honey in a soup pot. Bring to a simmer and cook until the plums are tender, about 20 minutes. Remove the sachet and discard.

Puree the soup until it is very smooth.

Season with lemon juice.

Chill the soup thoroughly.

Serve in chilled bowls, garnished with a dollop of sour cream and a scattering of toasted, slivered almonds.

CHAPTER EIGHT

accompaniments

CROUTONS ❖ CHEDDAR RUSKS ❖ RYE RUSKS ❖ BEAN AND CHEESE RUSKS ❖ FOCACCIA
(VARIATION: BREADSTICKS) ❖ OLIVE BREAD ❖ BUTTERMILK BISCUITS ❖ CHEDDAR CHEESE
AND WALNUT ICEBOX CRACKERS ❖ PEPPER JACK AND OREGANO CRACKERS ❖ GOUGÈRES ❖
PAILLETTES ❖ PALMIERS WITH PROSCIUTTO ❖ SAGE DUMPLINGS ❖ LIME GRANITÉ ❖
CANDIED ORANGE ZEST ❖ HARISSA ❖ PISTOU ❖ ROASTED RED PEPPER PUREE ❖ FRIED
SHALLOTS ❖ VEGETABLE CHIPS

M OST OF THE SOUPS IN THIS BOOK come with garnish and/or accompaniment suggestions but, as you become skilled at crafting soups, you may find that you want to improvise with these elements. Or, perhaps you already have a few favorite soups that you would like to play around with. This chapter includes recipes for several of the garnishes and accompaniments we recommended for some of the soups in this book, as well as suggestions for simple garnishes. These garnish and accompaniment recipes are as flexible as the soup recipes, so feel free to mix and match to your heart's content.

GARNISHES

Garnishes provide contrasting or complementary flavor and texture to soups, as well as providing additional color. Most garnishes should be cut small enough to fit in a soup spoon, so they are not unwieldy to eat. Large garnishes, such as dumplings or wontons, should not be so large that they overwhelm the cup or bowl in which the soup is being served. It is equally important that they not be too difficult to handle; they should be soft enough to cut through with the edge of a soup spoon.

Garnishes should be added just prior to serving the soup. If garnishes are prepared in advance, they should be cooled quickly and stored separately. Because serving temperature is extremely important for all soups, remember to reheat garnishes before adding them to the soup. The easiest way to do this is to heat garnishes separately in a small amount of the soup in which they are being served. Delicate items can be cut into shapes that will allow the heat of the soup to warm them thoroughly. (If they are small and relatively thin, they will not cause the soup's temperature to drop too severely.)

This chapter includes several recipes for croutons and other garnishes, as well as a number of other simple possibilities for garnishes. Small cuts of one or more of the vegetables used as the basis for a puree or cream soup can be steamed or boiled and used as a garnish. Similarly, shredded or diced meat, poultry, or seafood make an especially apt garnish for soups featuring these ingredients. Grated hard cheese, such as Parmesan, Asiago, or cheddar, or crumbly cheese, such as feta or blue cheese, can be stirred into the soup or sprinkled on top at the last minute to give a soup more flavor and body. Whole eggs can either be poached in the soup or beaten and stirred into the soup to form "rags"—as in the Stracciatella, page 24. Pesto made from any number of leafy herbs or greens (basil, cilantro, sorrel, spinach, etc.) or a puree of roasted peppers or garlic can be swirled into the soup. Whipped cream (flavored or plain), sour cream, crème fraîche, or yogurt can be dolloped on top or stirred into the soup. Garnish options for soups are practically limitless.

ACCOMPANIMENTS

Soups pair very well with other foods to become a satisfying meal. Even hearty soups that can stand on their own as a meal are enhanced by a hunk of good bread for sopping up the last of the broth. When it comes to pairing soup with other foods, soup and a salad or soup and a sandwich come instantly to mind but, as with garnishes, the choices are really limitless. From breadsticks and biscuits to crackers and vegetable chips, this chapter also contains a number of recipes for simple foods that make excellent accompaniments to soups.

croutons

This recipe makes enough croutons to generously garnish about eight servings of soup. Croutons keep well for several days in an airtight container, so the recipe can easily be multiplied. Cut the croutons into any size you would like, from tiny cubes for garnishing soups in cups to large cubes for soups served in soup plates or for salads. Just don't make them any bigger than a soup spoon, and remember to adjust the baking time appropriately.

MAKES ABOUT 2 CUPS $1/2$-INCH CROUTONS

3 slices white bread

1$1/2$ tablespoons melted unsalted butter or olive oil

$1/4$ teaspoon salt, or to taste

Remove the crust from the bread, if desired. Cut the bread into cubes. (If the bread is very fresh, dry the cubes in a 200°F oven, 5 minutes.)

Preheat the oven to 350°F. Toss the bread, butter or oil, and salt in a bowl.

Spread the bread cubes in a single layer on a baking sheet. Bake until golden, 8–10 minutes. Stir the croutons once or twice during baking so that they brown evenly.

GARLIC CROUTONS

Mince 1 clove garlic. Sprinkle with $1/4$ teaspoon kosher salt and mash to a paste with the side of a large knife. Add the garlic paste to the butter or oil before tossing with bread cubes. Bake as directed.

CHEESE CROUTONS

After the bread cubes have been tossed with butter, toss them with $1/2$ cup very finely grated Parmesan, Romano, or other hard grating cheese (a rotary cheese grater or a microplane grater will give you the finest texture and help the cheese adhere to the bread). Bake as directed.

HERB CROUTONS

Add 3 tablespoons chopped fresh or dried herbs (such as oregano or rosemary) to the butter or oil. Toss with the bread cubes. Bake as directed.

cheddar rusks

Rusks are slices of bread that have been toasted until they are crisp and golden brown. In France, rusks are called biscottes, *and in Germany they are known as* zwieback. *A topping of melted cheddar makes them extra tasty. Try experimenting with other cheeses, too.*

MAKES 8 RUSKS

8 slices French or Italian bread ($^1/_2$-inch thick)

1 cup grated cheddar cheese

Toast the bread until golden brown on both sides.

Preheat the broiler. Scatter the cheese evenly over the toasted bread and broil just until the cheese bubbles and begins to brown.

GOAT CHEESE RUSKS

Top each slice of toasted bread with a $^1/_4$-inch-thick slice of goat cheese. Sprinkle with chopped fresh herbs (rosemary, basil, thyme, etc.) or freshly ground black pepper. Heat in a 325°F oven to soften the cheese. Do not brown.

rye rusks

These rusks make a great complement to the Corned Beef, Barley, and Cabbage Soup on page 72, or the Mushroom Barley Soup on page 71.

MAKES 8 RUSKS

4 slices rye bread

$^1/_2$ cup grated sharp cheddar cheese

$^1/_4$ cup grated Parmesan cheese

1 tablespoon unsalted butter, softened

1$^1/_2$ teaspoons Dijon mustard

Pinch cayenne pepper

Remove the crusts from the bread. Square off the corners to make the bread slices rectangles. Toast the bread until lightly browned.

Preheat the broiler. Mix the cheeses, butter, mustard, and cayenne pepper.

Spread the cheese mixture on the bread. Cut each slice on the diagonal to make 2 triangles. Place under the broiler until the cheese browns.

buttermilk biscuits

As long as you don't overmix the dough, these biscuits will turn out light and fluffy. Mix the ingredients until they just come together to form what is known as a shaggy mass. If you have a convection oven, use it to bake the biscuits at 325°F for ten to twelve minutes. Try serving the biscuits with Ham Bone and Collard Greens Soup (page 59) or the Corn Chowder with Chiles and Monterey Jack (page 146).

MAKES 12 BISCUITS

1 pound all-purpose flour (3 cups)

2¹/₂ tablespoons sugar

1¹/₂ tablespoons baking powder

1 tablespoon salt

1 stick cold unsalted butter (¹/₂ cup), cut into pieces

²/₃ cup buttermilk

¹/₂ cup milk, plus more, as needed

³/₄ cup sliced scallions or chives, optional

³/₄ cup grated cheddar cheese, optional

Preheat the oven to 425°F. Blend or sift the flour, sugar, baking powder, and salt together.

Cut the butter into the flour until it forms pea-sized pieces.

Add the buttermilk, the ¹/₂ cup milk, and the scallions and/or cheese, if using. Mix just to combine the ingredients.

Roll the dough out to a 1-inch thickness on a floured work surface, fold over, turn, and repeat, 3–4 times.

Cut the dough into rounds using a 2-inch cutter, rerolling and cutting the scraps until you have 12 rounds.

Place the biscuits on a baking sheet. Brush with a little milk to make the tops shiny, if desired.

Bake until golden brown, 10–15 minutes. Cool on wire racks.

cheddar cheese and walnut icebox crackers

This savory version of an icebox (refrigerator) cookie is simple to make and goes well with many of the soups in this book, including the Clear Vegetable Soup (page 29) and the Fennel and Potato Chowder (page 154).

MAKES ABOUT 4 DOZEN CRACKERS

2 tablespoons unsalted butter, softened

1 cup grated aged cheddar cheese (about 2 ounces)

1/3 cup all-purpose flour

1/4 teaspoon salt

2 tablespoons finely chopped walnuts

Cream the butter with an electric mixer until fluffy. Add the cheese and mix well.

Add the flour and salt. Mix well. Blend in the nuts.

Roll into a log about 1 1/2 inches in diameter. Wrap well. Chill at least 1 hour or overnight.

Preheat the oven to 350°F. Line 2 baking sheets with parchment paper. Cut the dough into 1/4-inch slices and place on the baking sheets. Bake until crisp and golden, about 15 minutes. Cool on wire racks. Store in an airtight container for up to 3 days.

BLUE CHEESE AND PECAN ICEBOX CRACKERS

Substitute an equal amount of blue cheese for the cheddar and pecans for the walnuts.

index